TALKING TO STRANGERS

What To Know About Strangers We Don't Know.
A Stranger Can Be Your New Friend, But Not
Everyone. Learn Talking And Understanding
Strangers On Different Occasions.

By

DANIEL BRIAN

About The Author

Daniel Brian is an America based psychologist who holds a Ph.D. degree in clinical psychology. He has conducted many essential pieces of research in post-traumatic stress disorder, emotional regulatory disorders, substance abuse. He has practiced clinical psychology for more than 20 years and became a leading voice for many empaths and psychologist.

Being a passionate clinician, he stresses the need for psychotherapy in people suffering from stress disorders and he plays his part in excelling in this field. His line of interest was always human traits and how they affect their personality and regulate their emotions.

He also worked on neuroscience and related psychotherapy with neurologic aspects. His recent writings emphasize the evolutionary changes in the human brain which react with hormones and respond respectively.

This American psychologist stated that he was influenced by the field of psychiatry which tells exceptional stories and shows you the mental health of the individual. He combines his knowledge of emotional intelligence with neuroscience to demonstrate how to stay strong and powerful while being compassionate and empathic.

He included such stories in his book as he believed in emotional strengths that can regulate moods and feelings and also bought positive changes to many of his patients. His other works include empaths and healing soon after he realized the importance of balancing emotions and survival after trauma. As a practitioner of clinical psychology, he helps people out of the grip of their inner demons and encourages them to set healthy boundaries and know their sensitivities.

Table of Contents

INTRODUCTION--- 6

First Impression -- 11

Are All Strangers Your Friends? ----------------------------- 14

Things You Need To Understand ---------------------------- 17

Some People Don't Like Strangers --------------------------- 21

Why Do People Get Nervous? --------------------------------- 28

How To Improve Your Interpersonal Skills? -------------- 36

Why Are We Afraid Of Talking To Strangers?------------- 50

Things To Consider When Talking To A Stranger ------- 56

Respond to a Rude & Good Stranger ----------------------- 61

Build A Friendship With Good People --------------------- 64

When Is It Un/Important To Talk To Strangers?--------- 72

Unpleasant Conversation With A Stranger? -------------- 79

How To End Up Conversing With Strangers?-------------- 85

Stopping Your Kids From Strangers------------------------ 93

Kids Should Know Good/Bad Strangers. ------------------102

The Overall Experience Of Talking And Understanding
Strangers ---108

FAQS ---110

CONCLUSION---112

INTRODUCTION

Strangers are the individuals we do not know anything about or with whom we never interact before. Children face restrictions from parents when it comes to being in touch with strangers based on trust and several other factors. But in adulthood, talking to strangers is no longer an issue as we know the difference between good and bad strangers. In adulthood, people like to talk to strangers to develop new connections or relationships. Talking to strangers is always fun and exciting as it opens many doors to find many friendship and relationship opportunities. Many factors influence you while interacting with strangers. Do not take it as easy as it looks because you may get mistaken and fooled. You need first to differentiate the connection, then work on the personality you possess like eye contact, body language, smile, and way of talking.

It is necessary to be cautious that not many strangers give you a positive response. Sometimes you face the worst case because some people are so rude and stressed that they don't welcome strangers to talk and know them. You can find strangers anywhere, but few places can make it easier for you to find suitable connections. The places like the gym or walking track where you find many visitors with different jobs and ideas when you start talking to them may find a new friend. The other relevant place is the waiting area that is the best way to talk to strangers as they are getting bored standing or waiting in line, and they welcome you for the discussion.

The museum exhibitions, art shows, family festivals, or music concerts, such types of social events, bring many opportunities for you to meet and talk to strangers and be friends with them. Speaking and understanding strangers have many advantages because they open your mind and take you beyond your limit, family, and social circle. There are many benefits to talking and knowing a stranger.

1. Maximize your potentials

Many people have the same close circle of friends with the same perspective, educational background, and lifestyles. They share the same possibilities that restrict them from learning new stuff because spending time in the same group will not help you form new ideas or explore new things. The same routine, friends, and relationships will not let you see the world from different perspectives. That is why talking to strangers will help you get out of the same circle and discover new stuff because strangers will have other thoughts and ideas, different educational backgrounds, and lifestyles.

2. Find out your chance

Talking to strangers is great, and you positively can not identify who you might meet. For example, the individual running on the treadmill might have a job opening for you, so you never know what you get from a stranger. You have nothing to expect from strangers. Through talking to a stranger, can get you exposed to many opportunities.

3. Build New Perception

At times, talking to strangers assures not to lead to interactions like a new romantic relationship or friendship. There is a chance that you might get trolled and pranked. On the other hand, having one dialogue with them can be a revelation of their personality.

The stranger might modify your opinion and provide you with a new point of viewing things.

4. Improve your level of confidence

Most people avoid talking to strangers because of nervousness and anxiety. Keeping a lot of doubts in mind which can be the factor of not talking to strangers. To undertake this nervousness, you have to do the reverse of it. Improve the habit of meeting and talking to two or more strangers daily, then you will find a massive difference as it will boost your confidence level, and you would become comfortable talking to strangers. To improve your confidence level, you have to work on your nervousness; the more you get nervous, the more you will lose your self-confidence.

You don't feel nervous or uncomfortable even in social gatherings because you have learned how to interact or talk to strangers. Talking to strangers will give you the confidence to present yourself for specific purposes to the person like a date or a job interview.

5. Way to make new friends

Friends are a great support system whenever you need them, and they are there for you. In your good times or in bad times, they are there to share your moments. A good friend is also worthy of knowing your mental as well as physical health. Like a family, we don't have friends by birth, and they are also strangers before they meet you. You find some everyday things that attract you to make them your new friend. So to make new friends, you have to take a chance to talk to strangers.

6. Enhance your Social & Communication Skills

The main characteristics of successful persons are strong communication skills and good social skills. If the person doesn't know how to communicate or interact with other people, how can one deliver the ideas or products to the target people? So the social skills and communication skills are essential in both personal as well as professional life.

To enhance these skills, you need to practice it in your daily routine. Talking to strangers is the best way to practice these skills because it gives you a great chance to learn about small things, initiates conversations, has exciting and significant dealings.

7. Roadmap to treasure trove new friends

Talking to strangers will soon let you know the common likes and dislikes of each other.

Sometimes you might not find anything ordinary at all with the stranger you talk to, but the stranger may let you know about the person who has the same routine things that you possess. So talking to strangers can be the source for you to treasure and make new friends.

First Impression

The first impression when talking to strangers is usually influenced by body language and non-verbal communication. They set up that accessories, hairstyles, outfits, and additional features of a person's look have a minor effect on the first impression. Most of the studies indicated facial expressions and body language had reflected sound effects on the first impression. Talking to strangers is basic in everyday life. Even in the professional business line, you are familiar with strangers in new colleagues or new customers. In the educational ceremony, connecting with strangers is a top priority. Even in a standard societal site, communicating with strangers is a natural way to make new friends.

For an utterly confident person, talking to strangers is attractive; on the other hand, there is a small shade of nervousness always there while talking to strangers. As we know, it is the real-time to show the significance of making a first impression, as well as we all need to be admired from every communication. According to science, you made the first impression in the first seven to ten seconds when you meet any stranger. Enlisted below are the few points that would help you to form a good and positive first impression;

- **Introduce yourself**

The essential part introduces yourself like say hello or hi, tell your name and say nice to meet you within the first ten seconds. Try to give a productive verbal introduction so that others can remember your name and be comfortable with you.

Introducing yourself to the stranger and confidently talking to them will provide a positive impression as you want to be familiar with them, and it shows your interests in them.

- **Positive gesture**

Positive facial expressions can develop an excellent first impression. The best tool for positive facial expressions is a smile. People appreciate and feel comfortable with the ones who showed a soft and cheerful smile. Focus on it, don't smirk or give a broad smile indicating something wrong. Smiling is essential as it decreases the stress amount of hormones that can adversely influence your health.

In the meantime, the requirement to create a positive first impression can raise your anxiety level, and smiling is a way of a positive gesture to make it less severe. Smiling is the best way to start talking to strangers as it delivers positive vibes and gives an excellent first impression.

- **Communicate clearly**

Many people have great things to say, but they don't express it with confidence. That is an excellent reason for being ignored. You must be capable of representing yourself confidently and give every reason to get noticed. Don't overreact and become loud, whichever. It is better to talk to strangers clearly in a polite manner to understand your words and create a valuable first impression.

- **Proper Handshake**

A proper handshake can express self-confidence. You might be confused, but the appropriate handshake is an art. The handshake is recognized globally through a professional symbol of courtesy and politeness. Try to have a firm and proper handshake with the strangers that give them an excellent first impression and avoid a loose or uninterested handshake that negatively affects you.

- **Importance of body language**

Body language has a significant impact on developing a good first impression as it is the source of sending non-verbal communication. According to a saying, actions speak louder than words, so is the case here when you talk to a stranger, the first impression will be formed from your body language. Be careful about your body language that must give positive and polite images instead of rude and unethical conduct.

- **Have an eye contact**

Maintaining eye contact expresses that you are self-confident and attentive to anything they have to say. Eye contact reveals respect to the one you are with. It similarly expresses a sense of attention, and eyeing away a lot will mark you look diverted.

Are All Strangers Your Friends?

No, not all the strangers will be your friends, some strangers come once in your life, you won't meet and talk to them again. Some strangers don't have anything in common with you, so it is possible that you both won't be interested in being friends. Getting out to strangers, in addition to making connections with them, offers you opportunities to make new friends and perhaps come across your bosom buddy.

Some of the guidelines on talking to strangers need you to create a habit of talking to at minimum two new strangers every day.

Following are the conducts to shot the strangers into friends;

- Say "Hello or Hi" first because these are the magic words that break the significant barrier and initiate talking to strangers.
- Don't think about the result, as people worry about how the other person will respond and what if they don't show interest. It can be an insulting point for me. So avoid thinking about the outcome expectation, do what a reasonable person does, and respond to their choice and manners.
- Do not overthink the worst situation, and there can be chances that it will turn into a positive and respond to you more as you start the talk.
- You must have the ability to tolerate the refusals, and it is totally fine if the stranger doesn't reply to you or respond to you positively. It is their loss, not yours.

Think about it as an opportunity to learn how to face rejection and raise your tolerance level.

- Don't over jump to the conclusion, as everyone is different. There can be shy and reserved strangers who can't start talking openly in your first meeting. So don't take it hard and grant them some time to get involved in the discussions.
- The first time talking to strangers is always uncertain and awkward because anything you do for the first time will give you such feelings. Practice makes you perfect, and it is as true as it empowers you to deal with strangers and situations.
- Avoid asking too many questions while talking to strangers about their education, interests, and skills as they feel like being investigated. First, share your background, education, opinions, and interests and then wait for their response.
- Make some sense of humor while talking to strangers to create a happy and joyful environment. Most of the strangers want to relieve their stress by being with someone who gives them the reason to laugh and have fun. Beware of making fun of something that takes as a taunt.
- Find the things that a stranger wants to enjoy, like skating or badminton. They will show you their passions in their conversations, and you just have to find them and let them do it together.
- Smile is the source of attraction when you pass it to strangers to start the conversation. It will show respect and your optimistic nature and make the strangers talk to you.

The above are ways to change a stranger to be your new friend. As you start talking to them, you realize to make friends with that stranger because you find things in common. Talking to and knowing strangers doesn't mean to follow someone or to become cheesy. First, have some small formal talk. Then if you enjoy the company of a stranger, you can move on, otherwise, respect the difference and end up talking politely and formally.

Some individuals were looking to have an inherent ability for small conversation. Irrespective of the situation like festivities, career meetings, accidental gatherings, strangers during traveling, they can initiate a pleasant, free-flowing talk by any person and have a magical ability to create others' sense of attention-grabbing and extraordinary.

Things You Need To Understand

When you are going to recruit somebody for a job or meet a person for the first time, it tends to be hard to decide whether they are reliable or not. Regardless of whether it gives you a decent introduction, it may be false or misdirecting. To determine if an individual is dependable for an expert or individual job, you ought to watch their conduct and review their character through references and suggestions.

Observe the behavior of the person
1. The vast majority feel that it is understandable to state that an individual is lying by following the direction in which his eyes are moving. While lying, they will look upward and towards the left side, and if they are honest, they will look upward and to the right side. Keeping eye contact doesn't mean that the individual is coming clean, as the lying individuals don't generally look the other.
2. Whether a reliable person or a liar, your conversationalist will, in general, turn away when you act upon a problematic inquiry.
3. While eye to eye contact isn't the best way to decide somebody's dependability, an individual who looks is compelled to be a decent communicator and could be dangerous.
4. Focus on his non-verbal message. One sure approach to decide whether an individual is reliable is to consider their non-verbal communication just as how it looks.
5. Most confident individuals generally have open non-verbal communication, with their hands lying on their

bodies and their bodies confronting. Watch if the individual is folding their arms or facing you when you talk with them. This posture could imply that she isn't sure of herself and is not as attentive as you or hiding something from you.

6. People whose story is compelled to press their lips when taking an unsafe question. They can begin cleaning their nails, playing with their hair, or making awkward signals.

7. Watch if your conversationalist shows trust. Trustworthy individuals are usually accurate to show that they are dependable. If your guest is late without calling you to inform you or miss the commitment, it might demonstrate that they cannot show dependability. Also, if the individual changes the hour of the meeting without suggesting others or cancellation right away, it may be the case that he has no doubts about sitting around idly on others and that he experiences difficulty dealing with his time. In a merely expert setting, this sort of conduct is inconsistent, yet besides non-professional. If you escape the way with friends, it shows that the individual has no second thoughts about sitting around and may not be reliable.

Explore the character of the person

1. Go on interpersonal coordination. It is quite hard to keep up an intelligent presentation, particularly in this inter-connected world. Research has shown that an individual's Facebook profile reflects their actual personalities. If you have questions about an individual's reliability, check his records on various social networks, and check whether if they are real to the world.

2. According to research, many individuals regularly lie about little things on dating sites. They are trying to introduce themselves in an ideal manner, for instance, by telling lies about their weight or age to some degree or by increasing their salary.

3. Ask for at least three references or known contacts between you and the stranger. Get the individual for a proposed employee meeting or intend to contact them. You should ask for references at least 3 of them, including an individual connection and two expert references.

4. If your conversationalist is reluctant to give you his references, you should take care of it yourself. A trustworthy applicant would be glad to provide references in his resume since he would not be stressed over what that reference would say about him.

5. Pay attention to candidates who give you personal references, for example, a spouse, relative, or a close friend or associate. The best connection is an individual whom the candidate knows both professionally and personally.

6. Request other individual information, for example, your experience or a list of past businesses. In the case

when you are doubtful and uncertain about the individual's character, you can request that they give you more personal data, through the names of their past businesses or to do a little research on their background.

7. The names of the past bosses and their contacts can be utilized to confirm that the individual you are talking with is reliable and trustworthy and perfectly fits the post.

Some People Don't Like Strangers

Social nervousness is common. The feeling of being seen by others causes hesitation and concern. When we are the center of attention, we might fear the connection with others. Social anxiety has a few variations: stage fear, shyness, and social fear are the principal ones. Difficult to determine the reason for such behavior; we can identify genetics, family environment, education, and events. If, for example, you have been mocked in front of the whole class by a teacher because you did not know the answer, chances are there that you might feel difficulty speaking in public. It is essential to mention that we live in an atmosphere that features independence and performance.

HOW DOES THIS FEAR MANIFEST ITSELF?
The indications of social anxiety are different. In the spotlight, individuals regularly feel their heart racing, headaches. They sweat more, and they have disturbed stomach, look tense, and have dry mouth and throat. The terrifying side effects are those that reveal our anxiety. Becoming flushed, hesitating, and shaking are the main symptoms of it. Individuals have such appearances that show their nervousness and anxiety.

Anxiety casts us into embarrassing situations, and thus, we feel embarrassment and shame. This anxiety can even turn into panic attacks. To avoid such things, try to be calm and relaxed.

Hating Strangers Is A Part Of Typical Childhood Development

Research has been conducted somewhat about the connection hypothesis; it's the typical manner by which youngsters build up their security and vicinity to their communities (their moms specifically). Missing the point can imply that their ability to deal with relationships or trust will be destroyed. Human children begin to recognize the stranger for about five to eight months after meeting them. It is how their mind works.

The fear of Strangers Has Likely Also Been Culturally Developed — but We are Afraid Of the Wrong Thing.
"Do not talk to strangers! Even though our parents did not formulate this sentence, perhaps they spread the message in different ways. Why do we happen to be shy or timid? Shyness is another reason to avoid talking to strangers. This habit transpires all, in various ways, and to varying degrees. It's anything but an inquiry here of posting every one of the reasons. In any case, the primary driver can be summarized as one of the below factors:

Low self-esteem
This one is particularly valid for our secondary school experiences. It wasn't right to accept that our personality's kind characteristic was not intriguing, cool, or worthy of praise. We could attempt to adjust to everybody and not feel ourselves.

Too much self-importance

When others surround us, we become amazingly sensitive to what we do, as though people are around us. Feeling this increases anxiety and makes us criticize every one of our gestures and movements. Our focus revolves around ourselves and particularly on "what we did wrong." This behavior can trigger destructive behavior.

Boxing

By 'putting in a box,' I mean accepting to wear a label that defines us. When you label yourself as a shy/timid person, you feel psychologically inclined to respond to the expectations that come with it. In particular, "I am a shy person. I am like that, and things are as they are. When one labels oneself, one must respond to the expectations that this implies.

Overcoming Shyness/stranger fear: 4 Basic Principles

Before seeing these strategies and tips, I need to begin with four essential standards. They could be a procedure and tips shown below. However, as every one of these methods is optional, these four standards are necessary and inevitable. You can choose the ways that best suit you and create your very own plan. But you cannot select some of these principles and leave out those you do not like.

Be patient and perseverant.

To overcome this fear, don't be impatient and restless. You need to go slow. Getting great results can take a few months. Yes, I know, you didn't expect such a weak performance. What's more, that is not what you needed to analyze.

Overcoming shyness is a reasonable objective and a useful strategy. Yet, that can be a little time-consuming, like all self-improvement work. Also, the relapses you may face, and the confidence or inspiration drops.

Act constantly

Try not to open yourself to the incident that scares you the most. You will anxious and make the trip much more troublesome. Continue in progressive strides by placing yourself in a circumstance that stresses you a bit. For instance, if your fear is public speaking, don't go to a gathering at once. Start with a little casual introduction at work before a couple of co-workers. Gradually, by trivializing these circumstances that stress you a little, bit by bit expanding the trouble, you will figure out how to talk in the spotlight.

Understand your fear

Try to perceive what type of fear you have when and how you feel it in your life. Try to know what situation triggers this. Ask yourself what bothers you around then.

Overcoming strangers fear/Shyness: 12 Effective Techniques Since you have comprehended these standards, rules that you won't dismiss, let us go to the basis of this content: how to overcome it with 12 successful and safe strategies.

Obviously, the more you use these strategies, the better. Yet, this isn't a promise. Make up your list. Remember the four standards introduced previously

- Act slowly and patiently
- A progressive increase in the visible or recognized trouble

Move from self-concern to self-awareness.
Understand that the entire world doesn't take a look at you.
The vast majority is busy, taking a look at themselves. Rather
than observing yourself by someone else eye, look thoroughly
into yourself. Understanding what makes you shy and weak,
looking inside yourself will make you realize about self-
awareness. Mindfulness is the initial phase in any journey for
change or improvement in personal satisfaction.

Discover your qualities
we have many different qualities and ways of conveying
everything that needs to be said. It is essential to know and
accept the things we are good at, regardless of whether they
do not match the standards.

Recognizing one of the qualities encourages your confidence
and inner self, which better relate to you. It's a momentary
arrangement, yet one that will give you the confidence you
have to break the boundary of fear that you force on yourself.

Focus on others
Rather than focusing on your anxiety or awkwardness in the
evening, meeting, focus on other people and what they have to
say, try to know more about others, and invite them to talk.
Ask them questions, react to what they just said.

Try not to adjust to other people.

Trying to look like every other person is somewhat a good strategy but not engaging. Know that you reserve the option to appear as something else and to act naturally. Accept that you may not be seen as the most famous social individual.

Accept the rejection

Accept the possibility of being rejected and learn not to take it personally.

Do not forget: you are not alone to whom this happens. Rejection happens to everybody. It's life and the learning procedure.

The key is to manage adverse situations when they happen— being reasonably well prepared before it.

- Never think about it. It's not your fault. It is the individual's decision before you could have settled on another decision or another frame of mind.
- Find the lesson of this event: what did you learn? There is a good lesson in all happening. The possibility of improving your life is always there.
- Go ahead. Note when you are feeling frustrated about yourself, you are not pushing forward. It isn't by feeling sorry for yourself that you will change anything. When we begin to remember it, it turns out to be a positive response that we are not wasting energy while encouraging our morals by always looking for solutions.

Calm nervousness with relaxation

Nervousness and fear can appear to be overpowering if you train yourself to support more to overcome your feelings of anxiety. A beneficial method to quiet and manage uneasiness is to take a deep breath with your eyes shut and concentrate on relaxing. Breathe in and breathe out gradually while cleaning your mind.

Soothe nervousness through physical activity/sports
One way to overcome nervousness is to see it as crucial as vitality. Discharge the negative energy that chokes you by doing works out.

Physical practices like running or walking will help de-channelize the lost energy. It also allows you to escape the stress circumstance and change our perspective.

Meditate
Meditation will help you in various zones other than fear: stress, clarity of psyche, responsibility. It's something you do at least multiple times in your day. This habit will help you free your brain of the "negative influences" gathered, make you come back to a quiet and settled state, and consider the remainder of the tasks peacefully.

Why Do People Get Nervous?

When a person gets nervous while talking to strangers, it is quite familiar because everyone faces it. It's normal for them; however, it isn't, this can be an issue, and if a person doesn't learn to overcome it, it can cause problems. When a person is new to a situation or another person, he gets shy and nervous. While talking to a stranger, it is evident as they are unaware of how they would react or interpret the discussion and what might bug them off because they are utterly oblivious of their personality and behavior. It's normal when a person doesn't know a particular answer; it makes them nervous when talking to strangers; they get scared because they are afraid of falling prey to strangers. It's a natural human trait, a person is in a usual position, and they cannot find a way to overcome it.

People get nervous because they lack the confidence needed to talk to people. When a person is led to start a conversation with a stranger, they are afraid that they might not be able to deal with what's coming their way. The lack of trust between them and strangers and the level of comfortability is relatively low on every term. Hence, it makes the situation very awkward that's why a human has a variety of emotions and feelings.

Nervousness is also like a defense mechanism because they tend to defend and to sense the impending dangers and want to remove them;

We grow up in a household where we see people guiding that one should not talk to a stranger or even answer them because they might not have clear and good intentions, which isn't wrong because who knows what they have in their heart. When a person is grown with the thought process that strangers may harm them and constant questions in mind, it is hard for them to act normal around a stranger. A person can even start to panic around a known person that it can be understood entirely when it comes to a stranger; being an excellent public speaker is not everyone's trait.

Every human being likes to stay in their comfort zone. Being In front of a stranger can be similar; similarly, the advice of staying away from a stranger is so deeply embedded in our minds that when we think or encounter a stranger, we blank out. Our mind stops working, and our heart beats faster than normal. At that moment, being completely unaware of their whereabouts becomes a point where the stranger might look or seem like an opponent. However, one needs to understand that the stranger has not intended any strange vibe or negative attribute from their end. The person who is thinking of it that way and everything we are considering is based on assumptions and overthinking. False beliefs make a person nervous in front of strangers.

TO AVOID BEING NERVOUS AROUND A STRANGER, A PERSON SHOULD DO THE FOLLOWING THINGS:-

TRY TO UNDERSTAND THE STRANGER:
observe the stranger how they talk and concentrate on the conversation. Try to understand them and get to know more about them because the more the ice breaks, the more it gets easy to converse since the other person is new and unfolding few things. It makes it easier to think of what we can say because talking frankly makes everything easier.

SELF ANALYSIS:
Self-analysis, while talking to a stranger, is critical and beneficial at the same time. It makes it better and helps in the conversation, builds a more substantial impact on the stranger, and makes the conversation look better. For example, while having a conversation, do a self-analysis of whatever we are saying makes sense. It is vocal and robust enough for the other person to understand it.

It might kill the overthinking and negative thoughts of what the stranger might be thinking of us.

TAKE NERVOUSNESS AS EXCITEMENT:
When a person tends to be in a new situation In front of new people, they tend to be nervous as it's new, but new things can be useful since it is to be seen that being nervous if taken as excitement can make things easier.

STEP OUT OF COMFORT ZONE:
People should sometimes step out of their comfort zones and experience new things because it might be great for them. Similarly, while talking to a stranger, it might be new to them and entirely out of their comfort zone. It might build a great equation between you two because it might be awkward for a while, but you can make good friends after that.

TRY SEEKING PROFESSIONAL HELP:
Sometimes people can be so anxious and nervous that it can cause them panic attacks and destroy things. However, this can cause borderline depression. When a person thinks negative about themselves, they start to feel the inferiority complex. This complexity makes it hard for them to understand that it's normal to be anxious in front of a stranger. If they are unable to fight the nervousness battle, they should consult a professional help for guidance; talk to them about what can be done in this scenario, and overcome every problem.

BE POLITE:
A person should be polite while talking because it makes it easy for the stranger to be nice and comfortable. Being kind is necessary because when a person is polite, they are soft about situations and calm. Being polite makes the conversation light-hearted and not heated up.

AVOID BEING ALOOF:
A person should not portray them as distant and be less cautious about the conversation when they act like an aloof the other person also naturally acts the same way. However, when they talk, the other person might respond warmly too.

ACT FRIENDLY:

A person while talking to a stranger should act available; if the person acted strange or strict, it would make the other person stand on the edge, too, making the conversation hard to happen. Still, if they are friendly and approachable, it will make the conversation last longer. Instead of looking at the phone, staring at the walls, and looking around, one person should make eye contact to make it look like they are equally interested in the conversation. Eye contacts make the conversation better, as it seems like an impressive conversation. While making eye contact, a person should pass a smile and talk; it may make the other person initiate the discussion since the behavior will be completely friendly. While to look approachable, a person should work on their body language. They should not lean; however, they should have an upright posture, straight back, straight shoulders, and a steady head; this makes the person look confident, and the more confident a person looks, the more other people want to talk to them. Don't lock the arms on the chest or fold arms; this would make the other person think that the conversation is off and bored talking.

ACT NON-VERBALLY BEFORE INITIATING A CONVERSATION:

A person should first act non verbally before speaking because talking to an unknown person might look uncomfortable and strange. It can often look frightening, so before starting a conversation, a person should give signs that they want to talk to the other person.

Instead of just heading towards them and starting a conversation, a person should smile and make eye contact rather than just approaching out of the blue.

SLOWLY START WITH SMALL INTERACTIONS:
Talking to an unknown person is not easy. It can be tough to initiate the conversation, so before going and asking direct questions, a person should first start with small questions. So it doesn't seem entirely off to the other person, talk about the weather if not this, they should try talking about something common not to look rude ask about how they are, and how the place is, this would give them an idea that the person they are talking to is not rude.

GIVE AN INTRODUCTION:
Once you've nailed the small interaction, it's time to introduce yourself. Basic etiquettes revolve around to tell your name and then ask about others, or maybe they would generally tell their name once you tell them yours; this would make the impression of being polite and if the other person reacts with the same enthusiasm. It means they are interested in the conversation, too; otherwise, it will be pretty obvious that they are not up for a conversation. One should not try instigating the conversation.

ASK OPEN HANDED QUESTIONS:
While talking to an unknown person, it is very obvious that the conversation might gradually build up. The other person might be comfortable gradually, so instead of just hanging on to questions, and those answers last almost 1-2 words.

It might risk the conversation to fall off and not gradually instigate and start. However, it is necessary to make the conversation ongoing and not look short-termed to ask more open headed questions. These could include asking what they do, their day, and about their workplace, not looking desperate about it but generally asking about it.

MAKE THE OTHER PERSON TALK MORE:
Sometimes talking is necessary to make two unknown people at ease. The person should try that the other person speaks more so the conversation might last longer, look better, and get comfortable communication. Talking all by you might bore the other person. The person should ask about their expertise since this would make the conversation a lot about it, and this would also help them understand what the other person is trying to tell and more about them.

GESTICULATE:
While talking, a person should be open about a conversation, not make it look intense, and make it enthusiastic and friendly, and a person should gesticulate. Gesticulation is a way to make the conversation look energetic and makes the other person like us. When we try demonstrating the things with our hands and emphasizing more with our fingers and hands, this also has a good impact on our body language.

Talking to a stranger should be easy going and friendly; however, one should psych himself in making him liked on the first talk. Socializing is not easy these days because this is what happens. A person might be very shy and afraid while going to an unknown person and talking for the first time.

Behavior is the norm of society. It is the way people generally act while talking to different people in different scenarios; it is not necessary to act blue. The best way is to act natural and be you. A person should not talk about many things, such as what they should say or how they would look while talking. Instead of wasting energy on a person, we should try working in a basic conversational manner. Talking to unknown people increases our network and helps build a better relationship with people around us and be in good books because we never know that sometimes talking to a stranger might give us a new friend.

It also helps in looking at things with a broader aspect and with new intentions, and it may also help in better networking because having a wider social circle makes a person less lonely.

How To Improve Your Interpersonal Skills?

It is correctly said that an agent isn't only a representative; he is also a brilliant communicator. He knows how to deal, and unravel each one of the issues by communicating. Interpersonal skills are significant; however, they demonstrate your ability to use the imaginable thing as an extension and an asset. Let's understand why these interpersonal skills are substantial, and how might you develop them?

Why are Interpersonal skills necessary?

Know the standard, and indeed, the facts confirm that a person, who has excellent interpersonal skills and can use it both personally and in the discussions, progresses with regards to professional and personal lives.

With driving change, the world has become a global village, and we have lost communicational abilities, yet the businesses have known the significance of Interpersonal skills.

They search for representatives with excellent Interpersonal skills because that worker would be able to discuss productively with partners, associates, other staff individuals, and particular customers.

Here are a few ways to develop Interpersonal skills:

Have an inspirational frame of mind:
One of the significant parts of good Interpersonal ability is an inspirational attitude. It is one part, which can show a sequence of development in your conversations.

It is expressed that if you show an inspirational frame of mind during work, you are indicating respect for your work and the association for which you are working. Likewise, appreciating your associates' work, too, is considered an essential inspirational mentality.

Adapt simple ways to critical thinking:
A few people work hard day and night to take the organization to success.

If you are a part of such a situation, you may consider how quickly you take care of the issue or conflict. However, the problem is this may not be the right way to think. The perfect way is to determine the issues as it lessens the time and explains it well. When you are finished evaluating the methods to take care of the problem, you should continue and apply every one of the questions to understand it.

Ace excellent Interpersonal skills:
To pass on your message successfully use of signals are the ideal way to carry out the responsibility.

There are, mostly, two sorts of Interpersonal skills to be specific:
- Verbal communication abilities.

- Nonverbal communication abilities.

The essential part of communicating adequately is to listen properly.

You have to listen eagerly. "A suitable communicator is constantly a decent and insightful listener." Before giving your judgment, if you have listened attentively, you will know what you are saying and what the discussion is about.

If you get knowledge of communicating correctly, you are maintaining a strategic distance from the discussions, and you additionally increase your profitability. Be it non-verbal or verbal communication, both the variations are significant.

Verbal Communication: Verbal correspondence includes any communication, which involves words, be it expressed or composed. We have discussions with our collaborators, customers, or supervisors at lunch in a group. Verbal correspondence is a significant part of communication with regards to Interpersonal skills. However, you ought to know the significance of telling verbally well and become familiar with the art of conveying your message, because to give on what you mean in an ideal way is the best thing you can do to your colleagues.

Non-verbal Communication: It exists parallel alongside verbal communication. These two are beneficial assets, and together they can change the entire package of origination and recognitions.

Non-verbal communication, as indicated by reality, incorporates practically 60% of the open discussion you have with anybody. Non-verbal communication includes your non-verbal communication, facial expressions, stance, and how you make movements while communicating.

Your voice and the tone wherein you are talking likewise reveal a great deal regarding your style. Along these lines, you ought to also remember these points. The clothes you wear and how you conduct yourself is likewise a part of non-verbal communication. Non-verbal communication incorporates the following things:

- Eye to eye contact
- Speech and tone
- Dressing sense
- Non-verbal communication
- Posture

Add Inclusiveness to your work word reference:
You are not helping any secret departments of your nation, so instead of doing everything your way, figure out how to include every one of the people who are excited to work with you. Talking and listening to others' views is a lot; no one can tell which thought may take it to the next level.

If you work, you recover the co-activity, and you should ask the sources of info and opinions from your partners and associates in your working environment. A social amiability is required not just in the general public but also in the work environment where you work.

You should push and decide on social comprehensiveness before beginning any task. This condition will support your motivation.

Get familiar with plans:
The workplace isn't different from the places that you visit in everyday life. The board is a significant trait of the workplace and culture.

Certain things may offend or inspire you while you are on duty; at that point, would it be a good idea for you to respond? Obviously, no. So overseeing yourself and your feelings are a must for a stable workplace. Figure out how to control your disappointments and feelings successfully. When you have placed the self-administration work, you may effectively hide all the negative aspects. If there are opposite conditions, you should shroud these things to maintain a strategic distance from any adverse effect.

Start taking obligations:
One of the most crucial Interpersonal abilities is assuming liability and responsibility. The two Interpersonal skills are significant for performance and achievement.

If you have two qualities, you can do every one of the things easily. You are trusted, your collaborators will appreciate you. The one significant purpose of being responsible is that it helps in reducing tensions and conflicts between co-workers. Take this model, bearing your mistakes, and promising it that you will remember these things in the future will take care of issues.

Create social and overall mindfulness about things:
The best part of a talented professional is that he knows both socially and culturally. Here, socially implies the working environment culture you are a piece of. If you see, you unquestionably recognize the potential outcomes and opportunities. In a hurry to get achievement in your tasks, you may will, in general, stay away from people, which are harmful. If you have this nature of being socially mindful, you will recognize all the possible problems and resolve them effortlessly. Likewise, in an offer to be socially conscious, don't overlook different aspects of knowing more than what you should know. Try to gain from each movement and material things happening around you to improve your efficiency.

Try not to complain:
We see people complaining about their work and office all the time. A few people cry about their irritable boss, while others find their partners unhelpful. This mentality of yours doesn't hurt others as much as it hurts you. To create Interpersonal abilities, accept more and complain less. Thank your associates for their help that they have given to you. People love to relate and talk about stuff with a happy person. It is one action that doesn't cost anything besides makes the workplace incredibly positive.

Be more grateful:
An ideal approach to give your Interpersonal skills another high is to be more thankful for the people who work around you. It has two positive results.

To begin with, when you value some help somebody loans you or a work somebody has completed superbly, you are taken to be somebody, which recognizes the problematic work, respects their responsibilities, and praises them for it.

If you need any help, they will readily give it to you. Second, you signify the energy around you. By saying only a couple of thankfulness expressions, you add to someone else's result as lifting your very own Interpersonal skills. Aside from these central matters, here are barely any things that can be advantageous in helping you create Interpersonal abilities:

Be an Ardent Listener

When somebody is talking, try to be attentive and inspired by what they need to say or express.

If they feel that you are interested, they may likewise prefer to come up to you with their issues and understand your prospects regarding something, which would also support your Interpersonal skills.

Focus on Others

Although it is your work atmosphere or home, the essential thing that associates people with you is seeing that you give it a second thought and are interested in knowing what has been going on with them.

Attempt to Solve Conflicts

Clearly, with a working environment that treats such a significant number of people, there will be arguments, clashes, and battles. To build up your Interpersonal abilities further, you should be a dedicated communicator.

Attempt to sort through things in the workplace if there is contention and try to grasp people from a positive attitude. The significant thing to maintain a strategic distance from is chattering as it can make a realistic picture of you before people. Avoid backbiting as much as you can and never engage anybody who is associated with it, either.

Corporate leaders are acting unequivocally and contracting people who can help their associations' profitability. There are a few different advantages too as an expert, and, somewhat, these abilities may help you upgrade your own lives.

What to discuss when meeting strangers?
Conversing with strangers doesn't need to relate to pulling teeth. Take a full breath, think about a decent opening, and converse with the person! Try a frank "Hello, I'm [your name]!" Make a smart remark about something that is going on around you. Ask basic questions about where the person comes from, what they do, how they came to know a mutual friend of yours, and let the discussion usually bloom into something interesting. Keep in mind: the chances are that this person is also anxious about conversing with a total stranger!

Think of an opener.
In case you're going up to somebody and consider talking with them, you need a friendly exchange. A cooperative exchange will promise the person that you pursue expressive gestures, you're friendly, and are genuinely fascinated by them.
Don't generally overthink it. A basic "Hi, how are you?" or "Nice day, is this seat taken?" work truly well. Basic is best.

Try a touch of casual chitchat.

The casual conversation gets bad criticism, yet it shouldn't. Casual fun reveals to us a great deal about the other person and ideally prompts significant discussion. Ask the person what they achieve professionally and tell them what you do. Having a dialog about your employment isn't a fascinating discussion. However, it is intriguing to perceive what others perform for a living. Ask the person where they grew up. "Did you grow up here?" is a consummately fine-casual conversation question. "What was the city you spent your childhood in like?" is an incredible follow-up question if they didn't grow up nearby.

Ask about their sports. A decent method to outline this question is: what do you like to do in your free time?" Hopefully, they have exciting games and fun stories to tell. Don't discuss the weather, whatever you do. Rather than conversing about the rain or sun, try chatting with the person instead.

Instructions to Make A Good First Impression
Do you ever get worried when you are meeting people just because you harp a lot on what could happen? We, as a whole, try to be important. In any case, leaving a lasting impact on somebody we've recently met isn't, in every case, simple.

It tends to be genuinely nerve-wracking when you need to meet new people, regardless of what circumstance you are in. Irrespective of whether it is a planned employee meeting, meeting your accomplice's folks, or merely new companions and outsiders, it is hard to confront while feeling anxious.

Even though it is reasonable to build a decent connection, it may be difficult to tell how to do so. Let's discuss how you can create a proper connection; on the whole, how about we examine why we get so anxious when meeting new people. Here is a share of our preferred tips for making yourself important when you initially meet another person:

Put on your talking cap.
It's not difficult to remain there and let others carry on the discussion. However, you will never stand out in people's minds if you only listen.
Try not to give the fear of following a trick a chance to prevent you from screaming out and answering questions, relating to your own stories, and imparting your insights. Let it all out, and establish a long term connection.

Be blunt, mysterious, and genuine.
Many people avoid saying anything uncertain, particularly when meeting somebody, because they need to take no chances to guarantee everybody likes them. Yet, if you genuinely need to be important, you might need to create an impression without hurting anybody or saying something hateful.

Be novel.

Breaking out of the social standard is a simple method to stand out, yet try it positively. For instance, we recommend thinking of hilarious and different responses to the basic questions, for example, "How are you?" or "What do you do?" While thinking of scripted answers may appear to be torturous, we bring up that you should address these inquiries many times.

Use certain non-verbal communication.

Loot Riker says certain non-verbal communication performs more than make you look great; it makes you noteworthy. Having a confident handshake, standing upright, and keeping in touch both while listening and talking is a part of nonverbal communication.

Be connected with the audience.

We referenced earlier that you should talk and not react and listen to them. In any case, when you are listening, be mindful, and engaged.

The most prevalent and important people are those who give us their combined and complete attention. To make it clearer for you, you can do a few factors that you can do previously and meet another person.

Get ready for Questions And Talking Points.

Contingent upon the situation, it tends to be an excellent thought to set up your questions and things you will state in advance. It can be improbable if you are setting off to a planned employee meet-up.

It would then be able to assist you with being set up for any random questions or arguments. Furthermore, getting ready can help you with your very own reasonable understanding of thoughts and sentiments, making it simpler for you to examine a conversation.

Recall That Others Are Likely To Be Nervous Too
As referenced already, when you take the strength and weight off yourself, you can begin to see that it isn't just you that might be afraid. Other people who are meeting you are trying to build a decent relationship. Thus, they could be feeling similar to you.

When you begin to notice this, it can help you feel somewhat less anxious and progressively positive. It is because you can see that you are not the only one marginally stressed over establishing a decent first contact. Do whatever it takes not to focus on stresses and pressures independently. Understand that the people you are meeting likewise need to build a proper first contact.

Focus
When we focus on establishing the first contact and not looking anxious, we can sometimes lose focus around the most significant thing: what the other person is saying. Try and ensure that you are listening and focusing on what the person is telling you.

Smile

When constrained, Smiling can have an especially constructive outcome on how you and others around you feel. Smiles have emerged to improve our frame of mind and be irresistible to the people around us. It encourages everybody to feel positive and more joyful.

Furthermore, it can cause you to appear kind, so Smiling can help other people feel more enjoyable when meeting you. Although you don't want to smile from the start, do it at any rate, as the emotions you can get are still genuine. It can help you with feeling considerably more effective in meeting new individuals.

Dress Your Best

How you dress can genuinely improve or intensify your state of mind. When you feel low, you might need to wear easygoing, friendly clothes and not think much about your appearance. It probably would not be a good day to meet new people.

In any case, contingent upon the circumstances, how you dress and present yourself can genuinely help you with making a decent first introduction. If you are for a planned employee meet-up, ensure you have dressed fittingly, making you feel positive.

However, assure you dress how you feel good and that it makes you feel confident. It will help make it simpler for you to build a decent first contact.

Watch Your Body Language

Even though you do not know it, your non-verbal communication can genuinely show a great deal when meeting new people. A study demonstrates that non-verbal communication has more impact than anything you are saying when you meet somebody.

It incorporates eye-to-eye contact and eye-to-eye connection, showing that you are more positive and keener on the discussion. When somebody has excellent non-verbal communication, e.g., standing up with a big, firm handshake and great eye contact, they can be viewed as progressively confident, so this can help you with being less anxious when building your first connections.

Why Are We Afraid Of Talking To Strangers?

Many of us feel shy or reserved around strangers. What could be the reason for us to feel reserved and embarrassed around strangers? Is it fear or something else? We will discuss some of the reasons and causes below.

By Nature Disliking The New People:

Our mind has an evolutionary basis. Human minds tend to follow the lessons learned in the past. They become conscious and careful about the incidents they faced in the past and are afraid to have that kind of experience again. The main reason for this is the "fear of strangers." Humans used to live in groups or civilizations to protect themselves and have bigger resources in early times. They did not like to meet new people. Any stranger was taken as an invader and a threat to their security. So, it is a revolutionary cause of our psychology to dislike new people naturally.

- **Biological Causes:**
  According to a biological study, when we are around strangers, our body's cortisol level increases. Cortisol is a hormone that produces a stress response in the human body. It reduces the sense of empathy in humans. Correspondingly this makes us distant from strangers. It is the biological reason that we act different and weird around strangers.
- **A Normal Childhood Instinct:**
  It is normal in childhood to be afraid of strangers. Children are attached to their parents, any other person other than their parents is a stranger to them,

and they do not feel comfortable around them. Children tend to develop the fear of strangers from 5 to 7 months of age.

In an experiment, the mother was playing with her baby. Suddenly an unknown person comes into the room and sits with the baby. The mother then leaves the room. Baby and the stranger are alone. Then the mother comes again and plays with the baby. The baby's response at this time shows the attachment and love for his mother and the stranger's fear. The baby is happy to see his mother, and it is considered normal. It shows that the baby can differentiate between the parents and the strangers. It is not thought normal if the baby shows no response or does not seem to care at all.

- **Fear of Strangers is a Culturally Developed Thing:**
  The fear of strangers has directed towards the term, but it can be possible that we are afraid of almost the wrong concept. Their parents taught them not to go near strangers, not take anything from them, and stay away from strangers because strangers are considered "dangerous" for the children.
- **Social Phobia**
  Social phobia, which is also known as social anxiety, can also be one of the main reasons you are afraid or hesitant to talk or initiate a conversation with a stranger. Social phobia is the 3rd common mental disorder, and many of the cases are still not filed. So, the probability of getting a higher percentage can be expected. It is very necessary to go for counseling in this matter.

Because dealing with this situation can result in a social, behavioral, and emotional disturbance, it can hinder developing relationships. Finding support and getting yourself treated is the only help you can do for yourself.

- **Ways to Overcome Social Phobia: -**
  Social Phobia is a situation where you may find yourself disturbing when it comes to socializing or interacting with people. It can be a barrier for you to enjoy your life entirely. It is a situation where you think that you may speak something stupid or illogical, and you will make a fool out of yourself. By thinking this constantly, you will slowly get yourself detached from the people and make excuses for all the plans you have made with your loved ones. It can also stop you from developing any relationship, and you will be left alone doing your tasks. So, it is very important to treat this situation. Some ways to overcome social phobia or social anxiety are discussed below.

- **Challenge your Unnecessary Thoughts:**
  If you avoid speaking up in a business meeting or afraid to talk to a stranger at a party, you are experiencing social anxiety. The first step to overcome this anxiety is to control your unnecessary thoughts.

  These are the ones getting in your way to communicate. Overcome your irrational thoughts, speak with your friends or colleagues. Speak up your thoughts loudly. Do not hold back. Say what you want to say. If you are thinking or planning to say something or expressing your thoughts on something, speak up clearly.

- **Start Rating your Anxiety Level:**
  Another way to overcome your social anxiety is that you should start rating your anxiety levels around strangers.

  Rate 0 if something does not bother you at all. Rate 10 if you have a full panic attack due to something and mention that particular condition corresponding to your rating. In this way, you can get an idea about what makes you uncomfortable and the things that cause you anxiety.

  After you have made a rating list, then start practicing on the things which have the least effect on you. When you practice these activities, again and again, you will then get a hold of these, and after some time, you will realize that these things do not affect you anymore. When you have overcome these small fears, move on to the higher levels. Now practice these activities and overcome them as well.
  When you push yourself to practice these activities multiple times, you will notice that these things do not bother you anymore.

- **Start Practicing Meditation Yourself:**
  Meditate on your own if you experience social anxiety. Learn to take deep breaths in situations that panic you or make you feel anxious. Learning these breathing exercises will help you to calm yourself and lower your heart rate. If you have enough practice, you will become comfortable with these exercises. It is

something you can do easily if you find yourself in an anxious situation.

Another way to overcome stressful situations is to learn mindfulness. Mindfulness is something that has control over your mind and its activities. If you find yourself in an anxious situation, you can shift your attention to something more pleasant or something which appeals to your mind. Try to think of something more positive or something which makes you happy. When you have full control of the mindfulness activities, it can help you think about healthy things for you and your mind.

- **Talk effectively in a Comfortable Environment:**
  Suppose you are trying to get over the fears of talking in public, communicating with a stranger, or even initiating a conversation. Try to talk in a situation that seems comfortable to you. If you cannot speak out of your comfort zone, learn to talk more in your comfort zone. Contact a friend or plan a meet up with a person whom you are comfortable around. Talking in your comfort zone will help you to overcome your phobia.

- **Keep track of your Success:**
  Keep track of your anxiety level, and then practicing according to it can help you overcome your anxious situation. Another way to overcome your social stress and keep yourself motivated when you're feeling down is that you can start keeping track of your success. If you have done something unique in a social situation that can be termed as a success, you can record it as a success or something under the goal achieved. It will assist you to stay motivated if you lose hope.

- **Keeping a Journal:**
  Writing your activity during social anxiety is very important. Keeping a journal can also help track your activity and note down your success and failure, along with the reasons. It can help you sort out your thoughts and keep track of if you start to fall into your old habits again.

- **Stay Healthy:**
  If you are socially anxious or a person living with social phobia, you should focus more on your health and eating habits. Practicing healthy exercises and eating healthy food can also improve your mental and physical health. It will help you to get a hold of yourself and face difficult situations.

- **Love Yourself:**
  The most important thing for you to overcome anything, whether it is a social phobia or social anxiety, is to love yourself and take care of yourself. Do not be too hard on yourself. It does not matter if one day is bad, you have more to go, and there is still a lot to do. Be patient, be consistent, and never lose hope. Keep practicing to improve yourself and to overcome your fears. It is how you will succeed and achieve your goals.

Things To Consider When Talking To A Stranger

We have discussed some facts here that why people are reluctant to talk to a stranger. What are the factors or fears which stop them from talking to a stranger?
How can someone defeat that fear if that person has social anxiety and is hesitant to talk publicly?

Now we will concentrate on how to approach a stranger and start a conversation. How to respond to a rude stranger and how to respond to a good stranger. We will now focus on how to talk to a stranger without being awkward.

Body Gestures:
Whenever you approach someone, you do not know, and your body language speaks a lot. Whether if it is you or the stranger when you meet for the first time, your body gestures determine whether they or you want to interact or not. If they find you weird, they would probably not want to communicate with you, and the same thing can be applied to you.

If you want to initiate a conversation with a stranger, always try to approach the stranger with a warm approach. You can judge some things by the body language of a person if they want to talk to you. Or someone else can judge by the body language of yours whether you want to talk to them or not.

Always approach a stranger with open hands, real eye contact, and like nothing preventing you. You should look like you are not trying to hide if you want to talk to a stranger. Open hands indicate that you are welcoming them for a handshake, eye contact means you want to talk to them, or you are encouraging them to speak, an open body language shows that you are not taking them as a threat to you.

If you approach them with offensive gestures, they will not talk to you. If you have your hands in your pocket, it means that you are not welcoming them for a handshake. If you are folding your arms, it means that you are being reserved. If you are hiding behind something or are not maintaining eye contact, you do not want to talk to them. So, we can say that body gestures matter a lot when you talk to a stranger.

Opening Up:
As you have approached a stranger with a warm gesture, the next step is how you will open up to that person. Do not stress yourself out, thinking about what to say, what to not. The majority of the people initiate a conversation with a pickup line. They think that pickup lines are a better way to start a conversation. But this is not always the case, and some people get nervous with a pickup line.

So, a simple sentence to open up with a stranger can be, "Hey, how are you?" It could be it. You do not need any pickup lines or stress yourself out on thinking what to say or what to not. Asking them about their goodwill is enough for you to start a conversation.

Shake Hands:

It is good that you have come this far, you have approached the stranger, and you have also initiated a communication. The next step is to shake hands. It is always a good gesture to shake hands with people when you meet them, even with strangers. If you are not comfortable shaking hands, you should still do it.

Shaking hands build a connection between you and the other person because when you shake hands, your skin touches, and your body releases a hormone that develops a bond between you two. So, we can say that shaking hands is always good.

There are also some customs for shaking hands. Keep your hands dry when shaking hands because if your hands are wet, the other person will feel awkward or irritated. Always give a firm handshake; it indicates that you are welcoming and encouraging.

Introduce yourself

Now the next step is to introduce yourself and engage the other person in a conversation. A straightforward and familiar way to do this is by introducing yourself and asking about the other person. After the introduction, you can start a healthy conversation as of now you know each other.

A straightforward way to approach a stranger or engage them in a conversation is by offering help. It encourages a healthy and long-lasting relationship between 2 strangers. We have discussed how to talk to a stranger, and now we will come to an aspect of what steps you should follow to keep yourself and the other person involved and interested in a conversation.

Just Ask or Say What You Want to:
To avoid small conversations and to keep yourself engaged, do not think about whether you should ask something or not. Do not contemplate too much if you want to say something. Just say it. It is also essential that you should never forget the fact of being polite and within your limits. Remember not to invade their personal space. Still, you should ask appropriate questions and things without making the other person uncomfortable.

Do not Take Anything Personally:
When you are talking to a stranger, you do not know much about them, and you are trying to understand them better. So, a piece of advice for you is that you should never take anything personally. If you have asked something but did not get the expected answer, do not ask multiple questions of the same sort. It is just a process of knowing each other, and these things are every day. Try to make yourself creative, and your conversation is interesting. So, nothing bothers you and dampens your mood if you follow these steps.

Try to Make the Other Person Laugh:
To keep your conversation easygoing and comfortable, you should try to make the other person laugh or just bring a smile to their faces. Smile and laughter are the easy go factors of a comfortable conversation. If you make someone laugh, that person will positively remember you. Making others laugh or smile also keeps your conversation smooth.

Do not Expect the Outcome:

During a conversation with a stranger, do not expect the results. It could either be very good or exceptionally bad, and you are not responsible for it at all. It is just a conversation. If it goes well, it is good; you have had a good time with that person.

But if it does not go well, do not take it personally. Move on and forget about it. Just try to make that time easygoing and fun. That is all the purpose should be.

Share Stories:

When you are having a conversation with a stranger, note the common things in you both. Then prolong the conversation by sharing your personal stories about the similarities you both have. Ask them about their experience also. It is an easy way to keep the conversation flowing smoothly and fun without making anything awkward or boring.

Give Compliments:

Every one of us likes to hear compliments, whether we admit it or not. It is a human instinct to feel appreciated when someone compliments you. In a normal routine, we do not compliment others more often, even if they deserve it. So, try to compliment other people. It can help you to establish a healthy relationship. You cannot imagine how a single compliment can make someone day.

Respond to a Rude & Good Stranger

You are concentrating on the manners here. It includes how to start a conversation with a stranger, talk to them, and why people are hesitant to talk to strangers.

The other person's way of talking definitely affects you. If he talks in a good manner and leaves you with positive vibes, there is a possibility of a connection. If the person talks in a bad manner and deals with you rudely, it makes you feel bad and leaves you with negative vibes. You would immediately hate that person.

Responding a Good Stranger:
The ways described above are all that you can respond to a stranger in a good way. You can respond to them nicely and encourage them with a warm welcome. You can compliment them on their good traits and share anything common and good with them. Conversion with a good stranger is engaging and interesting. It seems like one person is encouraged and appreciating the other person to go with the flow and maintain a happy and friendly environment.

Responding a Rude Stranger:
It surely does not feel right if someone passes you a rude comment or deals with you inaccurately. It can ruin a good day for you and spoil your mood. It is necessary to withstand these situations by arguing back and fighting in public. There are some reasonable ways that you can follow to calm yourself down, control yourself, and deal with the rude stranger properly.

Ignoring:

It is simply the best and most effective way to handle a rude and unnecessary comment. Just ignore that person as much as possible. Do not let them ruin your day and spoil your mood. Ignore and walk away.

Defending:

Sometimes a rude comment can affect you deeply and emotionally. It becomes so much that you simply just cannot tolerate it and walk away. The solution to this problem is that you should defend yourself and make sure to do it responsibly. Do not lash out in public and start arguing rudely.

Tell the person they have done wrong to you, and you will not tolerate this kind of behavior.

Do not Let the Other have the Power:

Another way to handle rude comments is that you should answer the person in their way. Let them have the taste of their own medicine. It does not mean that you should start arguing in public or start to abuse. It means that you should not let them have control over your mood. Make them feel like their comment does not bother you at all and laugh at their face. It will break them and would be enough to silence them.

Do not Bend Down to their Level:

If you are on the right side, but you are shouting to prove your point, you would be considered wrong. Your valid point would be made invalid, and no one will believe or support you. If someone has talked to you rudely, you should handle it with a calm posture.

Do not go down to the level; do not start cursing or shouting. By doing this, the other person will always be at a lesser level than you, and you will be considered as a polite and controlled person.

Think About the Reason:
If you happen to experience a situation where a stranger has passed a rude comment to you, instead of getting hurt and calling them bad, evaluate the reason behind that comment. Think about what would be the reason behind the other person's behavior. Sometimes the other person is just trying to provoke you to start a fight.

Or it could happen because they are immature and do not have any manners or ethics; they do not know how to treat others, so they chose the way of being rude. Ignore the comment, think about the reason, justify yourself and forget about it.

These were all the reasons and justifications about the strangers. We, as humans, should always focus on the fact that nothing remains the same. Not everyone we know is good, and not everyone we do not know is bad. We should always focus on the good side and try to find the other side of the story. Sometimes people say something bad, but they do not mean it. In this case, we should understand and forget it. Sometimes people are just rude, and they cannot help it. In this case, we should just ignore them. It is not necessary that if a person is a stranger to you, they will be bad. It can also be possible that a person you know and trust can be a threat to you. Try to live logically and reasonably because this world is not for those who remain at the same place all their life

Build A Friendship With Good People

Human beings are social animals, society consists of a group of people living together and interacting with one another, and if we don't socialize, we will not survive. It's human nature to talk and make new relationships, build friendships, etc. But choosing the right kind of friends is important as friends impact our lives; you need friends who vibe your nature, understand and adjust together, who have a positive impact on your life.

They involve in your happiness, your daily routine, and your mental and physical health. Good friends make a person comfortable and bring them joy. Also, making the right kind of friends can have a good impact on your healthy lifestyle.

Friends who stick together for a longer period impact them throughout their life; hence, it is very important to make friendships that positively impact your life and make you happy and positive. You don't make friends within a blink of an eye, as it built overages. It requires compromise, tolerance, forgiveness, and many struggles, and it is not age-dependent either. You can make good friends in any part of your life, at any age, and it's never too late to build a healthy relationship.

Friendship serves several benefits;

- Enhancing your mood and having a positive vibe can elevate your mood positivity.
- Friends help you reach your goals. They allow you to focus on yourself by reducing stress and depression,

which affects your immune system directly; it reduces anxiety and depression in introverts—those who have problems talking to people and socializing.

- Friends just aren't partners of good times. They also help you sail through bad times, and they help you deal with issues much better.
- Good friends boost your confidence level and your self-worth. Friends hold each other during the worst and best of times, and being there for someone also comes up with happiness and a feeling of content.
- But you just can't choose anyone to share that kind of bond with other than friends. You need to ensure that you're completely comfortable with the person, someone you can trust and someone you can share your secrets with, and someone genuinely interested in whatever you are going through. You should look for someone who genuinely wants to help you through problems and accept you for your true nature, who doesn't judge you for issues and with whom you are comfortable.
- It is a two-way road, and you have to give what you take. Make the other person your half, be loyal, be there for him/her any time they want, and be sincere with their problems as much as they are sincere and honest with yours.
- A good friend should not assume stuff about you and judge you by things ordinary people would judge you for.
- Someone alright being physically comforting with you, especially when you're alone. A comforting hug, a

gentle, friendly pat on the back, and a push to move forward can surely play a major role.

Being around good and positive people will positively affect a person. It's your energy, and it's your value, your friendship. One should be picky about whom to spend their energies on and whether the person is worth it or not. You should surround yourself with sincere people who want to see you reach where you see yourself reaching.

Being around people having a good quality company is always good; one can not change the people around them and their habits, but you can always choose the people you want to surround yourself with.

One can only be as good as the people he's surrounded with; it's hard letting go of people you are close to, but sometimes these people can be toxic for you. We have to let them go on to healthy relationships, which can be one of the hardest things to do. But if one wants a positive change in life, they have to focus their energies on people who reciprocate their energies instead of avoiding them.

Good friends aren't angels, they are people like us, but they inspire you to become a better person; they help you achieve your goals and empower you to become the best version of yourself.

You ought to give off positive vibes and be confident. You should be yourself. This behavior will lead you to human beings, which might be reasonable for you. You can also practice forgiveness. Anger breeds bitterness and unhappiness, and it's time to let the negativity go.

"Sometimes, it's better to end something & try to start something new than imprison yourself in hoping for the impossible." – Karen Salmansohn.

We always know people who are exploiting us and are not healthy for us. Before sleeping, ask yourself how many people you met today and how many of them give you positive vibes. People who complain about you expressing your feelings, people who make you feel insecure, and don't appreciate whatever you do are the ones you need to cut off.

The primary step is to develop a healthy intellectual image of new people. Some of us see meeting new people as a horrible circumstance. We are concerned about creating a good impact on others and find opportunities for that.

If you consider the stranger's fear, ninety-nine % of people are afraid to converse with strangers.

While you're worried about the effect you are making, they're worried about the impression they will make.

The remaining 1% are individuals who comprehend that it is a good opportunity to build a healthy connection with strangers. Even if people select you based totally on what you do/say, are those people you want to be friends with?

Be open-minded. Don't assume

Sometimes you could have a lot of preset reasoning for the friend you want. Maybe a person who knows, listens, has the same interests, has similar educational records, etc.

Even as you meet the person and comprehend that he/she differs from your expectancies, you became distant. Don't do this. Give the friendship a chance to blossom. More importantly, give yourself time to develop a connection.

I have several excellent friends who come from actually distinctive backgrounds, and I could in no way have an idea that we are probably so close after I first knew them, actually because we share the same interests.

The word friend assumes to be excellent, which means pleasant to those who can understand its importance. Friendship needs to be cherished, strengthened and built for decades with super care. They encompass:

a) **Good listeners-** a friend needs to be a fantastic listener. If your friends feel that you no longer listen or have any interest in their lives, they will not confide in you. Without the capacity to concentrate, your friendship might be shallow.

b) **Being compassionate-** real buddies want to be compassionate continually. They have to sympathize with each other don't forget the problem their friends are going through.

c) **Loyalty-** actual friends are thought to be reliable. A real friend needs a tone with his friend no matter what. They should not betray each other.

d) **Support** – great friends must be supportive at all times. You want to have friends that you could rely on, and you have surety that he will have your back in every phase of life.

e) **Reliability** – a good friend is one that you could rely upon. All your friends should be reliable and honest.

Friends are folks that become part of their friend's happiness, and an actual friend is the one who usually assists them in their tough times. Loyalty is a critical feature of any friendship. Loyal friends typically care for each other's emotions and share secrets and strategies with no questioning.

Loyalty complements the purity of friendship.
Two people of any age organization can be friends, and they opt to spend time with each other. Share their secrets, suffering, feelings, happiness, and longings of life.

Ways to get rid of dangerous strangers
The stranger fear is a concept that has been taught to us since we were kids. It is an idea or warning that an unknown person approaching you could have dangerous intentions. It is a sort of experience nearly everyone goes through in their life, and what can we do to prevent that? Or avoid a situation that can be dangerous?

While you're traveling or watching for your train or bus to depart or on your plane to take off, try and chat with people, even if you assume they may be boring. It is valid mainly while you need to sleep at night in an informed station or an airport: there are chances to find a stupid companion than being prey for bad people.

- When a person continuously offers to help you or develop some components, make sure he is reliable. If you're uncertain, do not believe that person, so refuse the help with grace.
- Changing your place seems one of the super strategies to push away worrying about people.
- Dangerous and suspicious people are also present without hesitation and try to become friendly and may steal from you.
- Act uncertain as it may scare people around you. Nothing scares people more than an insecure person who seems to be loyal but is decisive.
- Engage yourself in a phone call, whether fake. This approach continually works, specifically at some time, when someone suspicious is around you.
- Run a long way from the man or woman if you suspect a few risky elements. No tips are as powerful as this one. If a state of events becomes too challenging to address, simply maintain your composure and move on.
- Don't react. Often people will trouble you to get a response. Try to stay away from them rather than panicking. Don't roll your eyes, make stern faces, or leave if possible.

- Remember that silence does not and never will make you weak. Take some deep breaths and control your respiratory system to calm yourself.
- Think about the bigger picture here: Getting right into a physical war of words can also cost you your health. Change the situation if you can. Some stressed people are courageous because they see the war of words as a war of egos. Once you've defused the scenario, they couldn't experience the need to say themselves.

When Is It Un/Important To Talk To Strangers?

Humans, being the center of the universe, are the most complex entity. They are so diverse to precisely categorize into species because you should know them correctly to order them all. Knowing humans with their true intentions has always been a difficult task. Even if you talk to a person daily, it is impossible to know him thoroughly, whereas judging a stranger seems to be a serious game. Many different important factors impact your talk to a stranger. You never know if they were, in the first meeting, comfortable enough to show you their real characters. But there are some parameters which help you to get a guess if the concerned person is right for you or not. Suppose you are going to with that person or not. To choose the right people for yourself to get something useful out of an interaction, you should know human behaviors, psychology, and nature. That will help you to save your time and stay away from toxic and unhealthy people. People who get a grip over human psychology can play with your mind and manipulate your opinions about them by changing their personalities accordingly.

Daily, You interact with different people. While talking to strangers, you must have some standards to judge whether this conversation is worth your time or not. What do they think while sitting alone? What makes them the person they are today? The people talk about the most significant things and their primary concerns.

If a person talks about some useful and creative ideas, this conversation might be worth giving a shot. Go for it, and try to learn something new from their experiences by listening carefully.

But if all that the other person talks about is how they met their girlfriend/boyfriend who they are going to break up within a week or fortnight, this conversation is not a worthy alternative to your favorite show. The worst and unbearable people just talk to explore other humans and show off their basic knowledge. Even if a person is talking about the most basic stuff, you may carefully listen to that. It is all about the vibes as your mind can figure it out when someone is making stuff or being pretentious. You might not get anything incredibly productive out of that conversation with those innocent humans who are too pure for this planet.

But it will always be the right way of catharsis and getting rid of the toxicity caused by the genius people. So above all, it is about the vibes a person gives you in the first meeting.

Talking to strangers can be relatively healthy as it will help you learn a lot daily. Even if you don't like the person or their ideas, you know something new about yourself by clarifying your perspective. When you talk to a stranger who seems to be friendly and intellectual in some rare cases, that's a jackpot. All you need is some effort to change them into a familiar person from a stranger. Keen listening is essential to know a person correctly, so try to listen more than you talk.

Rather than talking meaninglessly and adding to another person's points, try to listen to them talk and analyze. Make some opinions about people, but do not be too quick in judging people without even knowing them properly. Maintain eye contact while talking; to figure out when they are honest and when they are just making things up. Usually, people avoid eye contact while saying something not so real. But try not to make intense eye contact, so the other person feels embarrassed or uncomfortable. Do not preconceive a situation as any single point can change the meaning of the whole thing.

Just keep listening keenly. Make sure when you talk, the other person, instead of interrupting and continuously imposing their thoughts on you, listens and respects your opinion and views. Remember, a gentle person always listens carefully and keeps their mind open to new ideas and perceptions. A person is not worth talking to if he cannot accept different opinions than his own.

Generally, parents teach their offspring never to talk to strangers as their kids can not know their true intentions. In comparison, adults have built specific parameters on knowing whether to speak to a person or not. Talking to strangers always provides you some new lessons about what you should do and things you should avoid. But before speaking, you should always use introductory human psychology to choose which stranger to talk to. While talking, observe what the significant concerns of other persons are. What do they talk about most of the time? Is it the ideas and some concepts or something about their daily routine?

Communicate to strangers who speak of something new that you didn't know before, or something that can change your point of view. Seeing things from different viewpoints and breaking the boundaries you have created around can broaden your mind and perspectives. Doing this can help you a lot in your dealings as you will become more accepting of new ideas.

Talking to strangers will help you overcome your social anxiety. The more you get to know people, the more you will find them different in different aspects. These differences exist because of various factors that affect a person's personality in life.

Every individual has a different, unique point of view and perspective to see things. Mostly, brought up the environment and circumstances they have gone through influence these perspectives. Perspectives matter, the position from where you watch the situation dramatically affects the things you see. You might see the world from the high mountain of privilege you have been raised on. Talk to a stranger with a somewhat different background than yours, and you will find a completely different perspective of the world from yours.

Talking to strangers can give you some general knowledge about things. Carefully listen to the cultural or traditional talks as you might need or utilize that knowledge someday. A healthy discussion on some important stuff like politics, fundamental beliefs, current affairs can change you into a different person you never expected yourself to be.

That one talks and one moment of revelation might bring meaning to your life. It might make you realize your destiny and where all these events are taking you to. So, talk about the universe, how wide it is, how it works, and how our existence affects its functioning. How you find Donald Trump funny, and how is he ruining politics. Talk about concepts and notions of doing something great that might help you achieve your mission or goal.

Being around a specific group of familiar people will not let you grow as a person. You will just act and increase depending on your judgment of how those individuals want you to behave. You will behave as you have already been programmed and trained by your brain. This behavior depends upon your observation about the personalities.

Talking to one stranger is much more beneficial than talking to ten familiar people as the former will make you come out of that shell you have created for yourself. You analyze, observe, and learn about different human behaviors and change your stagnant personality for yourself. Talking to a stranger will help you to learn about and deal with new human actions. The more you talk to strangers, the more you will learn about social psychology. You will create a general idea about how people react in different situations and circumstances and how they are supposed to respond. It will also help you with your relations in life. You certainly learn something out of every discussion, and your personality will develop with each interaction.

Talking to strangers doesn't just build confidence in you, but talking to the right ones can benefit your physical and mental health. Talking about things and incidents that you feel embarrassed about can be purgative for you as there will not be a fear of being judged or left behind afterward. It happens because people do not behave genuinely due to the fear of being judged and being left in that idea their friend might not like. That fear of abandonment never lets them be who they are and show their real self, and that guilt of not being the person they want to create a sense of hatred for themselves. That feeling just keeps piling up there until the person can no longer bear themself. So they talk about it to a stranger and be who they are, even for some time.

The right choice is far from straightforward: Most of us prefer to avoid getting hurt and feel embarrassed. There will always be a fear of rejection and being judged whenever we are talking to a stranger. So we avert our eyes, zip our lips, and keep it all to ourselves. However, we also know that these people are our most significant source of happiness, so there's an enormous potential to get out of our comfort zones and take that social risk.

So, better to put down your phone for a second, plug that hands-free out, and smile at a stranger. Start a casual conversation with the person sitting next to you—console a classmate who is going through a tough time or never talks in class. You never know what you might learn from it. Probabilities are, you're overestimating the amount of awkwardness and terminating the potential feelings of joy and connection of these small meetings.

As William Butler Yeats said, "There are no strangers here, only friends you haven't yet met."

So, go talk to strangers regardless of what kind of person they might be. You will always end up getting a good lesson out of it. Just take care not to waste time on the stranger you once did and let them stay a stranger if they are not helpful for you, anyway. You will not get anything productive out of it, even if it can enhance your anxiety. Avoid talking to people who just want to impose their authority and make you feel inferior to them. Communicate with people who feel like sunshine and who talk about more important things in life.

Unpleasant Conversation With A Stranger?

Talking to strangers might not always turn out as you expect it to be. Some people are entirely different from you. But that is not the problem; the problem is the non-cooperative and rigid people about their beliefs. They just try to prove you and your beliefs wrong try to impose their views on you. If by any unfair chance, your day starts with such talk, those arguments have the power to ruin your whole day or maybe traumatize you for your entire life. You might feel it difficult to talk to a stranger for your whole life because of that one experience. The argument can be as small as the kind of ice-cream flavor or the working best politician. People must have the tolerance to accept other's beliefs and ideas. Talking to a stranger can help you to be flexible about your thoughts. When you observe human diversity, you start accepting that humans are different from each other. They believe in different things, and it is OK. There is always a reason behind what people think, and you should accept that as you cannot just deny what their beliefs are. They built those facts through their life experiences.

No two humans can be completely similar; everyone has different beliefs. You must give each other the necessary space as everyone has faced different situations and went through various circumstances. The environment brought up dramatically affects one's choices and beliefs. It is quite rare for two humans to have similar life experiences as their understanding of life will differ because of how life treated them. Intolerance towards other beliefs is one of the significant reasons for disharmony and anarchy in the world. If people just start accepting each other's ideas, life would become much more comfortable. There is no need to adopt those beliefs; just don't oppose and belittle them.

Keep your beliefs intact and do whatever you want unless it doesn't affect someone else's beliefs. Be more accepting of others, and the same will come back to you, as you will get what you give. That is how society works and keeps going. When someone is talking to you about their belief, that means they trust you and asks you to accept them. Suppose they share a problem, asking for honest advice, talking to them, and being that compassionate life-changing stranger for them.

It is not necessarily what you believe in is always the ultimate truth and the right thing. So be open to new ideas, learn, and adapt to new situations. When you understand, the other person also feels comfortable around you and talks to you more friendly. It will help you understand human psychology because people will share things with you, and that will also strengthen your relationship. Being open will also help you groom your personality. A rigid person will not learn from others' beliefs and perspectives as he/she will be too busy denying others' experiences and proving themselves right. Such people will always suffer because of their rigid beliefs and cause anxiety to others as they have already created a firm image that they are not willing to change at all. They are too egoistic to innovate themselves with the new and dynamic needs of the ever-changing modern world. Such people are just too weak and shallow inside to accept other's judgment. They just want to hide their insecurities in any possible way and want to exercise the power they never exercised on people with weak and vulnerable beliefs. They misuse people, whereas those who are not insecure never execute such tactics to inflict their authority.

A self-aware person and has expertise will never do anything to belittle others' opinions and outlooks. They listen to people and give them good suggestions. Even if they are not able to do so, they will just listen carefully with full attention. Such people do not make anyone feel inferior based on beliefs. A knowledgeable person knows about human experiences, and he/she knows how fine-tuned a human being is and what to say in a particular situation. They keep that sensitivity and human nature in mind before speaking anything that can hurt the other person.

But there is a significantly low probability of meeting such people quite often. This whole world is choking with crack heads and speed freaks. What will your reaction to meeting such a person? If you are an internally weak person who is already insecure, you might start cursing him and yourself. You will feel bad like a loser about the discussion. Just after the interaction with such a Mr. Know-it-all, a feeling of despair will surround you. You might feel like a setback to yourself—a person who cannot even be valid enough for themself, a person who is tongue-tied and all others are better than them. You might feel like someone who has no purpose, the most worthless and insignificant creature on this whole planet. Anyone can come and crush you beneath their foot like you are a burden to this world. You will begin to think of yourself so lowly that you will deny even the talents and expertise you have in yourself, a person who cannot affect anyone or anything in this unified world, existing silently, and is going to die one day. This one bad experience can traumatize your whole life, and others like you will feel the same in such situations and circumstances. The person saying this might not even have a realization of what they have already done to you. They might never be able to recover the sufferers from the trauma of never being good enough.

For an aggressive and outspoken person will meet Mr. Know-it-all, this may cause some severe consequences. There is a significantly higher chance that they will just keep opposing each other, even after being wrong, just for the sake of influencing the debate to prove themselves right. They will just keep arguing to keep their ego intact. For an egoistic person, dropping an argument might seem to be a matter of life and death, and they would go to any extent to keep their dignity intact. That interaction can get offensive and turn into a conflict as both will be the quacks quacking at each other. They will just shout at each other without any knowledge of what they are saying or doing. A person who doesn't have sufficient knowledge to prove their argument right raises their voice and harsh their tones to prove their argument, but it would have no use. It might only work if one person is different from another, but when both the people are the same, and on fire, it can only result in destruction and grief.

When a knowledgeable person communicates with a stranger who will just be bluffing about things to show him/herself right, the literate person will prefer not to argue. And if he/she does engage in an argument, they will first listen and heed to all that Mr. Know-it-all has to say and then put ahead of their point and try to track the other person with their arguments giving reasonable conclusions. But if the other person wouldn't agree to their point, they will not force it on them and make them accept their point. A knowledgeable person never thinks of his/her ideas as the best and undeniable. They know that there is always some fault in things, and nothing can ever be perfect, not even an idea. Such people accept realities and facts just like they are. Hence they are always open to new ideas and transformation. They have enough control over themselves not to let people direct them or drive them crazy easily.

While talking to strangers, you should be more flexible and accept the changes and human diversity. Be eager to learn something new every day. Be a bigger, better person, and try to be the best version of who you can. You can make so many mistakes, but the key to success is making errors and learning from those mistakes.

Accept people and their heterogeneity, be more open towards other's beliefs and concepts. For you, others' opinions might not be as right as your beliefs, they might not be the untarnished right and best, but you are not the center of the universe. Sometimes you should respect the differences as they can unite people. Not everything starts and ends at you; what you believe in is not the ultimate reality. Get over it; above everything, perfection does not exist. You can also be wrong sometimes, so accept these facts. There is no need to change your beliefs, but do not deny others' beliefs. In case you don't agree with them, tell them that it is not always necessary to agree on everything. Do not beat people for not having similar opinions like yours.

They might be the beginners and in a phase of learning and developing their ideas, as you were doing someday.

Remember that everyone has a different pace, and the velocity doesn't determine their success or downfall. There is always something special and unique in every person. All individuals are special in one way or another. They might not be like you, but that's how human beings and this whole planet functions. Respect the existence of differences. Try your best to learn at least one new thing from every stranger you meet. But meeting that stranger again is up to you. You have to figure that out for yourself, whether to make that outsider familiar or not. Ultimately, it is your choice; it will become what you will make out of it. Being human, you are superior to all the species on this planet. Get something out of your superiority and utilize it to bloom hearts.

How To End Up Conversing With Strangers?

It is conceivable to end a discussion effortlessly, says Morag Barrett, an HR advisor, administration mentor, and creator of Cultivate: The Power of Winning Relationships. Recently, I shared some of Barrett's tips for starting a systems performance discussion. Here are her tips for consummation one politely:

1. State thankyou and farewell

In some cases, the most modest methodology is to be immediate. "it has been remarkable conversing with you. Much obliged you for yielding your experience. Appreciate the remainder of the night." Barrett recommends going with this statement with a handshake (except if either of you is adjusting nourishment and beverages) and afterward proceeding onward.

2. Ask who else you should meet

"I guaranteed myself I would reach three new individuals tonight. Who might you recommend I talk with straightaway?" This methodology works especially well if the individual you are conversing with knows many others on occasion. They may even make an introduction to help things along. On the off chance that they don't have a suggestion for whom you should meet and talk, say thank you, and proceed onward, Barrett exhorts.

3. Introduce the other individuals to somebody you know. It is the other side of the last proposal, Barrett says.

"You are starting the new bestowal, and once you have done as such, you are allowed to proceed onward.

4. Ask headings to the restroom
"A basic reason and a sign that the discussion has concluded," Barrett says. Be the as it may be, do make a straightaway for the restroom and not the bar to maintain a diplomatic distance from any misunderstanding or offense." According to her, it is the best possible and gentle excuse to leave a talk.

5. Offer to convey a beverage.
This one isn't among Barrett's tips, yet it's an idea I have utilized regularly to end a discussion on occasion. State something like, "I would go get a drink. Would you like me to bring you something?" This polite offer will almost continually meet with a bountiful refusal, however on the off chance that the other individual takes you upon it, it's sufficient to bring the beverage, state something like, "I truly appreciated selecting you," and proceed onward.

6. Inquire as to whether you will meet the other individual at a future occasion.
I have genuinely appreciated chatting with you. Will you be at the following gathering? Perhaps we can proceed with our discussion at that point. As Barrett says, this is quick and painless and welcomes future associations. It likewise flags that you have to move onward until further notice.

7. Request the other individual's card.
Now and then, the most straightforward approaches are the simplest, "Barrett says. "Request a card, take a glance at it, and thank the individual for their time. Requesting a card shows

that you have liked this meeting and want to further remain in touch. This tip is a way of giving honor. There is a chance that a person may ask for your card. In that case, be polite to share it with a facial expression of happiness and gratitude.

8. Give the other individual your card.

If that person has not asked for your card, Barrett suggests saying something like,

"Let me give you my card. If you don't mind, connect on the off chance that I can help you in any capacity, that would be an honor for me." If you don't need the other individual's card or the person in question does not offer one, at that point, show yours. It's a usual sign that the discussion is on end," she says.

9. Request to associate via web-based networking media.

If you communicate with a person and feel that they are best for you and want some further meetings, try to get connected on networking media. Barrett prescribes saying something like, You have contributed much to invest energy with me. May I interface with you on LinkedIn? That would be a pleasure for me. She likes to ask for consent before sending an identification request, even though it may not be carefully vital. Contingent upon your management and whether your manufacturers and new colleague is progressively a business agreement or an individual, one may request the interface on Facebook or some other interpersonal organization. It's a decent way to flag that the present discussion is finished, yet you might want to keep in contact, like requesting a card.

10. Plan a social gathering.

On the off chance that you and the other person might work together, or you might want to warm up to the person in question, at that point, ask as to whether the person might want to meet for espresso at a future date. That will provide you two a chance to converse with fewer delays.

What's more, it also recommends you proceed onward for now and find other exciting individuals to begin new discussions with. It is a sign that you are starting a journey of a new friendship.

You can consolidate or utilize these tips that might be independent, relying upon your circumstances. Some apply both to the eye to eye discussions and those led via telephone. It's all about your ease and requirements.

Have a reasonable plan at the top of the priority list, regardless of whether you are setting off to a company, a systems executive occasion, or the washroom. Have an urge at the top of the priority list for what you need to accomplish. Would you like to meet an elegant woman? Or void your throbbing bladder? You are contrasted between possibly offending someone by continuing onward and needing to accomplish in a different way at whatever point you are caught in a discussion. Having a sensible reason at the top of the priority list for what you need to complete encourages you to make leave lines and talk about underneath. It enhances your ease of communication.

Sit tight for a break in the discussion. "Well." "Alright." "In any case." "So." Such words arise when a conversation has quickly slowed down. They're defining moments where you can start a new subject. Sometimes the discussion itself attracts a nearby topic. Accordingly, they're the ideal chance to end the conversation and begin to separate. They will say "So," with an upward cadence in the voice, assured of the discussion's extension. You answer with a tone of more downbeat conclusiveness, "So." And then you immediately change into your leave line. "In this way, tune in. It's been remarkable getting up to speed with you. "Bring the discussion around to the description you connected in any case. Feelings of similarities initiate the bond. Whenever the situation supports, this makes for a smooth completion. If you started the discussion by approaching somebody for their plan for a class to take? Then end this meeting with, "Well, I welcome your tip. I'll certainly try to get into that class during enrollment." Or if the meeting started with somebody approaching you to take care of an issue at the workplace? Close the conversation with, "So I welcome you drawing this problem out into the open. I'll certainly send Jim an email this evening to make knowledge of what's happening."

Utilize a left line. As I described earlier, this is the place having a plan which genuinely makes a difference. With regards to what sort of leave line to employ, first, be frank. Manufacturing pardons is attractive; however, it can resemble to be irresponsible at the time and lead to more issues later if reality gets out. Second, put the accentuation about what you have to achieve. It makes your exit look less similar to the other people's judgment– like it's not about them; there is simply something you have to do. Here are a few instances and examples of these leave lines (likely imported by a "Well..."):

I have to get a seat. I need to utilize the restroom before the start of the motion picture.

I have an inquiry I have to pose to the speaker before the end of the working hours.

I have a cutoff time I have to meet before the early afternoon, that is why I must return to work.

I think we should try to make proper acquaintance with everybody here.

I made a target to meet three new individuals today before evening time.
Now I should go to the kitchen to make something for the kiddos. Then I am going to see the Romantic workmanship show before it closes.

While concluding the discussion, which you have started, attempt a line that carries conclusion by suggesting you have checked something off your list ("simply" is your best companion here):

Along these lines, simply state that you wanted to make sure everything was alright.

They were simply required to perceive how the new position was going.

If the other person started the discussion to take help or to request counsel, finish up things by asking:

a) Is there something else I can assist you with?
b) Is there something else you require?

In some situations where the above leave lines aren't suitable, then virtually hang tight for a conversational defining moment and say something like:

It was extraordinary getting up to speed with you.
Anyway, it was an immense pleasure to see you once again.
Utilizing the past tense in such lines tells the other individual that the discussion has found some conclusion, and you are almost to leave.

Another kind of generally good leave line is something like:

- Anyway, I would prefer not to corner all your time.
- Thank you so much for your time.
- Indeed, I would prefer not to keep you from your work.

I'd just utilize the overhead lines; you can also use them at the end of your discussions, just like they need out, or you actually can't consider anything to state. They can appear to be somewhat bowing – all things considered, on the off chance that they genuinely opposed you taking as much time as required, aren't they equipped for saying so themselves?
You also risk them bouncing in with, "God help us, I wouldn't disturb by any means!" and the meeting progresses forward.
At long last, by and large, when you hear such lines from somebody, they register as an escape endeavor. It means that the other person will end the meeting, and you are going to get departed.

Carefully head to your end. Fine contends that "The cardinal guideline of the exit is that when you leave and end your meeting, you do what you have promised." If you state you have to discover a seat before class begins, though, then walk ten feet and start communication with another person, your abandoned discussion associate is going to realize you lied and dumped them. So, when you excuse someone before ending a meeting, make a genuine one. Similarly, on the off probability that you state about a conversation with another person, they see you turning erratically through the gathering looking lost. They are going to feel hurt, which is a normal human response. Individuals will take note; everyone gets hurt by deception. Try to leave with a conscious reason to do what you said you expected to do.

As a last resort, you can generally make the essayist George Plimpton, who always hefted around two beverages on occasions and parties. On the off chance that he wound up fastened in an undesirable discussion, he'd courteously remove himself by saying he is supposed to convey the other beverage! In this way, he gets out of the meeting without hurting anyone. That is his own way; you can make your own according to different situations.

Stopping Your Kids From Strangers

At the point when you are out with your small kids, multiple times, sociable outsiders frequently approach you to grin and make proper acquaintance. Even though you like your children to be affable, you additionally need to show them not to speak with outsiders. It is quite an awkward situation, where you can not hurt the outsiders and want to convince your kids solidly. How might you abstain from sending mingled messages?

"Try not to speak with outsiders" has been the standard for some parents for ages. Be that as it may, it's a smart understanding for children to talk with outsiders now and again. Communication builds confidence in the talk, and they also learn to speak to others in different ways according to situations. In case of emergencies, when you are not around, how will they communicate with strangers? Who else will they go to on the off chance that they're lost and need support?

Along these lines, rather than making a standard, it's smarter to instruct kids when it's proper and suitable to talk with outsiders and when it isn't. It's better to tell them the ways of communication. When your children are out with you, it's fine to give them a chance to make proper familiarity and converse with new individuals. You are viewing the circumstance and will ensure them on need.

However, if your youngster is distant from everyone else and brought closer by a more strange person, that is an alternate story. It is worth a discussion thing about you and your child.

Tell your children that if an outsider ever approaches them and offers a ride or treats (like sweets or toys) or requests help with a task (like helping locate a lost canine), they should step away, shout "No!" and leave the place right away. Be attentive to those who are getting close without any reason for doing so. Your youngster should let you know, or another confided in the grownup (like a trainer or childcare specialist) what has happened.

The equivalent goes if anybody — regardless of whether a more unusual, relative, or companion — requests that your kid stay quiet about, attempts to touch your youngster's private region, or requests your kid to touch their private parts.

Most children will probably be careful about outsiders who are mean-looking or seem alarming here and there. Be that as it may, most youngster molesters are standard looking individuals, and many make a special effort to look social, agreeable, safe, and speaking to kids. Rather than deciding on an individual by appearance and looks, this way instructs children to pass judgment on individuals by their activities. Ask them to notice the actions of these people without getting diverted from their looks and words.

It's additionally critical to ask children to confide in their very own impulses and zones. Instruct your kids that if somebody makes them feel awkward or feel like something's merely wrong, they have to leave the place right away regardless of whether they can't clarify why. There is no need to find a reason why you are not answering a neighbor. You are not supposed to do that if you are not comfortable with the situation or their behavior.

What if your children are distant from everyone else and need to move toward an outsider for help? Guide them to start with; they should attempt to discover an individual in uniform, similar to a cop, security watchman, or store representative. If there are no formally dressed individuals, search for grandparents, ladies, and individuals with kids who might have the option to help. Do not panic; try to relax. What's more, once more, remind them about impulses: If they don't have a positive sentiment about someone, in particular, they should move toward another person. Or they can shout for help in a public place where several families and couples are passing. If they gain public attention, then they are in a safe zone.

It's impractical to shield kids from outsiders all the time. However, it is credible to show them fitting practices and what to do on the off chance that someone goes too far or is trying to harm your children. Remembering these tips can enable your children to remain safe while they're all over the place.

We have the capacity as guardians to misrepresent thoughts when we show our children, mainly when showing their wellbeing. We utilize appealing expressions like "more odd threat" or "don't talk with outsiders" to urge our youngsters to be aware of potential risks. While the goal is admirable, it might cause more catastrophe than anything. In this article, we'll reevaluate how to converse with kids about wellbeing by clearing why more bizarre risk isn't the best strategy and concentrating on the best way to instill certainty, as opposed to fear, in your kid.

Father strolling with youngster

The more exciting threat doesn't show your kid security; it instructs them doubt. The expression "more abnormal hazard" attempts to paint wellbeing in highly differentiating ways by telling your kid that anybody they don't know is risky. Lumping all outsiders into the dangerous class can give your kid a misguided feeling of weakness when they experience an outsider all alone. Much of the time, there is a chance that they're lost, undermined, or somebody is tailing them—the most secure thing your kid can do is approach an outsider for help. You can set up your kid for these situations by showing them the contrast between great outsiders and awful outsiders. When they are aware of different types of personalities, they would judge the strangers and manage the situations.

There are great outsiders and terrible outsiders.

Encourage your kids to be careful of anybody they don't have the haziest idea; however, don't educate them that all outsiders are awful. Kids consider outsiders uniquely in contrast to what we do. Keep an eye on the persons who are communicating with your kids. Consider who your youngster associates with every day. Who they consider being an outsider might be unique about what you think.

My sibling and his family live in Seattle. We see them perhaps two times every year for family occasions and occasions. When my sibling attempts to converse with my three-year-old, she responds as though they were a pack of scorpions. In any case, when we go to the bank, she'll talk with the teller like he's family since she sees him consistently. Sometimes, the children don't think of some people as strangers, as they are continuously seeing them regularly. It's you who tells them about the definition of strangers.

Do I know or trust the bank employee? Not past essential budgetary exchanges. Would I leave my little girl with my sibling at the end of the week? Totally. However, if I had the bank employee and my sibling stand next to each other and asked my little girl which one is more abnormal, she'd state my sibling since he is new to her. At three years of age, she doesn't get a handle on the idea of trust as we do, so all things considered, we're instructing her to perceive great outsiders that she can request help.

Who is a decent, more unusual?

Help your youngster recognize trustworthy outsiders and terrible outsiders by concentrating on what they can search for. A decent, more unusual is somebody your kid can request help if they need it. Accept the open door while you're out in the open to bring up examples of good outsiders for your kids.

Alternate and have them work on appreciating great aliens to you so you can figure out their judgment. Make sure to underscore that they shouldn't move toward just anyone.

By rehearsing with your youngsters, you are imparting surety. You're engaging them to realize how to shield themselves from the threat by identifying and reaching a decent, more abnormal. Remember that there's no idiot-proof strategy to know somebody's goals just by taking a gander at them.

Females are not always safe, and males are not always a threat to them. Try to find a safe zone on moving towards a couple with kids or many families when there is no guard or cop aside. Show your children to be wary, in any event, when speaking with great outsiders, and stick to specific security and defense rules.

We did an investigation to discover which metro townships have the most police and firemen in the U.S.

What makes an awful, more bizarre?
An awful, more strange is somebody who attempts to get a youngster to achieve something without their parents' consent. Shockingly, it's not as simple to bring up terrible outsiders in broad daylight. Yet, you can advise your kid with some basic notice signs to recognize a horrible person more interesting:

A grownup requests that they oppose their folks or accomplish something without asking permission.

You should guide your children to be supplanted or just avoid outsiders. Ask them to take permission or let you know before going anywhere or when a stranger is calling them or asking them to do something. Guide your grown-up kids that it is essential to immediately inform you if anybody makes them feel awkward or requests that they stay quiet. Explain to your children that the grownups can do their tasks independently; there is no need to help them. It's alright to state no. It's necessary to get my permission before you go anyplace."

Conveying obviously and explicitly to your youngsters about your desires again ingrains trust in them. It's not fair to always tell them about the negatives. Just tell them the acts they should avoid. Disclose to them what they ought to do instead of what they shouldn't do.

Basic wellbeing rules for children and guardians:
Trust in yourself. On the off chance that something doesn't feel right, seek help immediately. Littler kids may depict this as an "oh dear" feeling. Trust those emotions and find a parent, instructor, or other great outsiders to help.

Ask your kid to always stroll with a companion. Terrible outsiders search for kids who are distant from everyone else or their caretakers. Walking with other children will assist them in remaining safe. When the kids move in groups, no one can dare to harm them, as a single stranger can not handle a group of children. So keep you in groups while outing.

Guardians conversing with kid
Ask your children to remember their names, guardians' names, home addresses, and telephone numbers. If they need to locate a decent odder for help, they can call your folks or the police for you. Knowing your name, mother, and father's genuine names, address, and telephone number can enable a decent, more forward helper to get you securely back to your mother or father.

Privileged insights aren't protected. Commonly terrible strangers attempt to utilize the mysteries' approach to test your boundaries and capabilities. Tell your folks immediately if somebody requests that you stay quiet about it. State: "No, I don't keep insider facts from my mother and father."

Play the Freeze Game if you're lost. Ask your children if they get isolated from their folks out in the open; they should solidify where they are and trust that their folks will remember their means and return. On the off chance that anybody attempted to assist you with letting them know, "I'm playing the Freeze Game until my mother and father return. Will you remain with me?" If this individual attempts to compel you to move, question, and tell.

Holler and tell. If you are alone and somebody attempts to take you, shout as noisily as possible, "This isn't my father; he is trying to take me somewhere!" Tell your folks or another great odder quickly on the off chance that somebody tries to get you to go with them.

Utilize a family code word. In some crisis circumstances, you may require a companion or neighbor to get your kid. Your child may think about that individual as an outsider. Having a family code word can engage children to settle on the correct decision. Have them stay away and request the code word. On the off chance that the stranger can give the code word, your youngster will realize that they are sheltered; the person came from their parents. If they can't, advise your youngster to hurry to wellbeing and discover a decent, more unusual.

Locate a decent odder. I've referenced finding a decent odder is the most secure alternative and helpful on a large scale. Advise your youngster to utilize what they've penetrated and located a decent, more interesting individual who can support them. At whatever point, they feel compromised or get an "oh goodness" feeling.

Openness is of the utmost significance, yet at times it's difficult to tell where it began. Have a go at breaking the ice with a kids' book about safety. As children love stories, telling them a story can make their concept about threats and safety measures.

Kids Should Know Good/Bad Strangers.

Who is a stranger?

A stranger is a person that your family is not familiar with. Strangers can be of both types, good and bad, and children should know to differentiate between good and bad strangers. Children have a different perception of strangers. Usually, our kids have a picture in their mind of a stranger being the one who has scary looks like villains in cartoons. This picture in our kids' minds can be dangerous because strangers with pretty looks can be equally vicious.

Whenever we talk about strangers, we talk about both men and women. Though the media portrays stranger dangers and people who abduct children as men, women are seen just as much as men to be abductors, so we need to be aware of anyone unfamiliar to the child or the family.

As parents, we should specify things to kids then 'just do not talk to strangers.' We should ensure that the children are aware that a stranger can be a person who resides just a few doors down; it could be someone at the supermarket, someone at school, a neighbor, or another friend's mom and dad. We should make sure that our children are aware of the happenings of our society. They should be familiar with criminals' tactics and have some necessary precautionary measures to save them in case of isolation.

What makes a good stranger?

A good stranger is a person to whom your child can approach whenever he needs assistance. You should help your kid to differentiate good strangers from bad ones by concentrating on specific features. Whenever you are with your kid in a public place, point out to people you think are good strangers, and on your next visit with your kid, ask them to identify good strangers with the help of signs you taught them in the previous visit. Make sure you teach your child that they should not approach just anyone they see. Groups of couples are always better options to take help than the one or two strangers passing by.

Teach them to remember easily recognizable strangers like a cop, a security guard, a parent with a child or children, teachers, principal, librarian, or someone at a grocery store or shopping center with a name tag and is possibly an employee.

It should always be remembered and kept in mind that there is no definite way of knowing someone's intentions and aims. However, helping your kids distinguish between good and bad strangers prepares them to stay cautious and take straightforward safety rules if a mishap happens or in care of emergencies.

Who is a bad stranger?
A bad stranger is someone who does something with a child without their parent's consent. They can do things that can make your child uncomfortable or frightened. Unluckily, it is very difficult or almost impossible to point out a bad stranger in public places. But teaching them what goes on in society can help them to safeguard themselves when needed. Ask them that if a stranger tries to touch you, tell your guardians.

It is suitable for your kindergarten or playgroup age kid, especially if they are going out, to learn safety regulations with grownups that the family does not know. You should make your kid realize that adults should not need to ask them for help to do their tasks independently. Adults should not give them food or treats if they do not become familiar with them. The strangers should not ask them to come into their houses or get into their cars even if it is raining or something else.

The kids should not accept rides from strangers. And if any adult tries to touch your kid or make them feel awkward and unsafe, your kid should be able to realize that they can always say no, and if the adult is making them feel afraid, they should flee and yell and then should tell somebody about the experience they had. It is probably best that parents just keep the right eye on their children and not put them in surroundings where they might be exposed to a stranger, and something atrocious could occur. As they grow up, they can distinguish between good strangers and bad strangers better by using their extinction.

What are the possible stranger dangers?
Stranger danger is the term usually used for something dangerous that a stranger can do to a child. Bad strangers commonly harm kids in three ways: abduction, injury, and assault. Kids are taken from places like school bus stops, from their houses, and the stores. Injuries can occur both physically and sexually that go along with assault. So those are all things you should be regarded about when talking about strangers and children.

Children of what age are at risk of stranger danger?

Children from all age groups are prone to stranger danger. Abduction, injuries, and assault is seen from infants up to the teen years, so we should ensure that our children are aware of stranger danger even when we think they are too old to talk about stranger danger.

At what age should I talk about stranger danger?

It should probably start at four or five years with just some simple stuff. You do not have to get into it that it makes them nervous, but start talking about who strangers are and a stranger is somebody that your family does not know. Tell them some social incidents and crimes about stranger danger and how they should react in such situations.

It is always OK to reassure your child that it is alright to talk to someone new, mainly if you are present with them, but if they are not with anyone and an adult address them, they should get attentive and behave towards them a stranger.

What are the safety tips for children and parents?

To help your children discover who is a stranger and a friend, especially when we are talking about pickups after school or sporting events or activities, we should specify that person's name, perhaps who they are, and what they look like, what kind of car they drive. You can even develop a code word that adults can share with your child, so they know the person exactly who is supposed to be picking them up.

Tell your children that secrets are not safe for them. Many times bad strangers ask children to keep secrets from their parents. Teach your child not to listen to them and to share everything with parents for their safety. Do not judge your children, be friendly to them in such matters, so they would share all their problems with you.

If an abduction occurs, teach your children to yell and tell people around, or if someone tries to make your child feel uncomfortable, teach them to run away from there, and share with good strangers and parents about his wrongdoings.

What steps should be taken when any mishap happens?
If an approach happens
If a stranger approaches your child, the first and foremost thing to do is connected to the police division, call 911 promptly, and collect as much information regarding the stranger as you can. It could be any type of clothing that that person had on, any marks, any scars, any tattoos, hairstyles, hair color, type of car they got into, and what color car is the information is required to be shared immediately. Try to provide all the information you have about them.

Missing/lost children
In case if your child is lost or missing, call 911 as soon as possible. We always encourage parents to have a current picture of their child in their wallet, including their height, age, weight, hair, and eye color. It is essential information that will help assist the police department in finding your child even faster.

What can be the possible effects of stranger danger?
Stranger danger can have severe effects on families and children. It makes parents limit their child's outdoor physical activities and make them stay indoors, resulting in making

kids isolated. Fear of stranger danger does not allow parents to let go of their child to walk alone to school. They have to take some extra responsibility to pick and drop them at school. A child's self-capability is reduced a lot because of this. They quickly get panicked and confused in isolated situations. Parents should pay massive attention to kids as sexual abuse can profoundly affect kids throughout their lives. The consequences can be low self-esteem, developmental disorders, emotional difficulties such as sadness, depression, rage, drugs and alcohol problems, etc.

Last Words
Never let the communication barrier stand between you and your children as the communication barrier can result in serious outcomes. It is highly unlikely that something terrible happens to your child; however, you want them to stay cautious and aware that there is a risk. Teach your children to be attentive, even when talking to good strangers, and stick to the basic safety rules.

The Overall Experience Of Talking And Understanding Strangers

The overall experience of talking and understanding strangers and encountering other people could be overwhelming. Getting to know them and understanding them could make it better to interact as we react according to our understanding.

Strangers could be very helpful or very terrible. Understanding what a person demands or what's their nature could help us deal with them better. Your child should know about creating boundary lines and distance, cutting people off with a smile, or tricks to avoid stranger danger.

All of these could be helpful, but getting to know more people and making friends could be a new experience. Walking to work, taking a bus or a tram, and sharing your daily route with the same people can make you good friends. But talking to strangers and understanding what kind of people they are is crucial because you never know what kind of hostility they bring. They could be criminals, thieves, or smugglers. They could be dangerous or life-threatening.

But walking up to an unknown person and starting talking or initiating a conversation could be challenging. It could be an exciting thing to do that requires experience, but it could also be risky.

It needs practice and confidence. One can always learn different communication methods by practicing and going to social events by themselves, practicing in front of a mirror, or asking a friend to help you initiate a conversation. It can be overwhelming but can also help them overcome their fears. Hence dealing with strangers can be both comfortable and complicated depending on how good you are at it.

FAQs

Frequently asked questions about dealing with strangers are:

1) how to avoid a person who seems dangerous?
Well, for that, you can turn the person down simply either by telling them you have to go or by pretending you're busy on your phone or something. Wearing earphones can also be restorative as they don't talk when they feel ignored or notice you're not interested in talking to them, so ignoring can be one of the significant things you do to avoid talking to a person.

2)What if the situation starts to get out of hand and you're alone?
If you ever feel like the stranger approaching you is dangerous and can cause some kind of strain you cannot deal with, the best thing you can do is run as far as you can until you reach some safe place. While running, shout out for help. It's the safest and quickest thing you can do.

3) how to avoid strangers altogether when you know the person has wrong intentions?
If someone is approaching you, you can pretend you don't speak that language. It can completely shut off the person as they won't be able even to begin the conversation.

4) how to teach your children about a stranger?
One of the important things you face is dangerous people approaching children as they are easy to target. You can't completely stop your children from socializing or talking to people, but you can teach them things that can help them deal with something better. Also, make sure when you're teaching

your kids about strangers, you don't frighten them of people as it can have a lot of negative impact on their personality. Make sure your child keeps you posted and shares about whatever is happening. Earn their trust, and make sure they're comfortable telling you if someone is approaching them in any way. Tell them how to avoid strangers, also let them know if someone's picking them up from school, they should tell them some kind of codeword only you and your kid know. You need to strictly observe your child's behavior around people and make sure they're acceptable yet careful.

CONCLUSION

Meeting strangers come with a lot of good and bad things. How you deal with things is the real deal. Approaching people could be as hard as skydiving, and if you're bad at it, it could make you feel lonely at celebrations, parties, or public events. You sometimes need to approach a stranger to have company. And sometimes it's the opposite. Sometimes you have to avoid a stranger for being too noisy at a bus stop or while going to work. We often deal with people who are just too clingy and get into our personal space, and you can turn them down with a smile or by pretending you don't speak the language. Show yourself busy on the phone or start avoiding them, and using headphones while traveling can also be of great help to prevent a stranger. Sometimes, some situations get dangerous, and you need to have safety measures for those kinds of problems. Keep sprays of some sort with you in case of an emergency and make sure you remember to run. Running away from danger is the best thing to do when you don't have anything or another person to help you with.

As much as it's unusual, don't panic; if you use your brain on time and avoid the situation, you can get safe from any unwanted problems. But just not only elders. Children are the most exposed people to stranger danger, and one of the major concerns of parents is to let their kids be safe when they go out. Children are an easy target for criminals.

So teach your kids not first to take any edible things from strangers. But also don't scare them off as it can kill their friendliness. Ensure your kid trusts you enough to tell you if someone is approaching them with negativity or risk. Teach your kids some self-defense if in such cases and tell them how to avoid talking to bad strangers too.

Especially during school time, let your kids know not to go with anyone until they share some secret codewords.

As a grownup, approached by the wrong people could be upsetting and can make a person feel vulnerable. So dealing with it wisely can help you get a hold of yourself and the circumstances.

Dealing with situations quickly and on the spot can help avoid any kind of stranger danger. It also can improve your confidence in yourself.

Made in the USA
Middletown, DE
02 May 2021